'The voices of people with more profound learning difficulties are missing; no kind of access enables them to be heard directly in a book using symbolic language...

... we must hear silences too.'

Jean Searle & Melanie Nind

(2009)

Understanding and promoting access to people with learning difficulties. Routledge; London.

An Introduction:

This book contains the ascribed (and therefore, I freely admit, somewhat speculative) musings of a middle-aged man named Harry. I have known Harry, on and off, for well over thirty years; firstly, as one of his professional carers, then as one of his special education teachers, and after that, well just as a friend I suppose.

However, I don't want to say too much here, not in this introduction, as what I would really like is for Harry to tell his own story … but the harsh and simple truth is that he can't; not in a way that you, the reader, or I might understand. Yes, this very stark reality means that Harry will never be able to tell his own story, not directly, not in his own words. Actually, not in any words, not ever, not for as long as he lives. You see, he just isn't capable, not now, and nor will he be at any point in the future. You see, he just hasn't got it in him, words that is, and he never will.

But that doesn't mean that you shouldn't get to know Harry or Harry's story; to get to know something of his life. No, on the contrary, it's because he can't tell his own story, in his own words, which makes it important. Yes, it is important to spare him some time, to give him just a little time to get to know about his story, and about his life.

So, who is Harry?

Well, Harry is a man with a profound intellectual disability who has lived all his life in a special hospital or in residential care. Now, having a profound intellectual disability is something that is really profound; it profoundly effects everything. It profoundly effects a person's ability to learn most of the things that most of us take for granted, even the simplest of things. So, despite being nearly my age, now well into his sixth decade, Harry hasn't yet learned to talk; no, not at all. In fact, Harry still hasn't yet managed to utter a single meaningful word, and the unfortunate truth is, he never will.

There are various terms used to describe people like Harry. He is sometimes said to have a profound intellectual disability (as I have done above) or profound and multiple learning difficulties, or he is sometimes categorised as someone with complex needs or complex and multiple impairments; that's a lot of labels for someone, anyone, to carry around with them everywhere they go.

Other people, yes, other less charitable people, may use much less kind words to describe Harry, but we will let that lie for the moment. But whatever words others use to describe him, Harry would be said to have an Intelligence Quotient or IQ well below 25 (according to the generally accepted ways of classifying such things - although these classifications aren't necessarily accepted as accurate, useful, or even ethical by everyone. Certainly not Harry, he couldn't care less about such things).

The 'average' person, like you and me (for argument's sake here I am assuming that you, like me, are fairly average, so please don't take offense), well our IQ would be expected to come in somewhere around 100 - although to be honest, when it gets as low as Harry's the idea of an IQ becomes pretty meaningless really. At this level, a person's IQ can't actually be measured (if it is actually a useful 'measure' for any of us, either side of the average 100. And really, the people who might try to do it (with such people no doubt claiming to have very high IQs themselves), well to be honest, they're just having a bit of a guess. They may say it's an informed estimate or it has a wide margin of acknowledged error, but really, between you and me, it is actually just a guess. And anyway, it doesn't really help any of us either.

Anyway, I digress. So, Harry can't talk. He never has; not even one solitary, single word. Although to do him justice, he may recognise his own name. He probably does; although, in reality, we can't really tell; but yes, he probably does. But Harry can't, and hasn't ever, audibly volunteered a single symbolic word; not a word that can be represented and expressed in our socially shared, recognisable, symbolic form of speech. He hasn't as yet, despite his now quite extended life said a single thing. No, not in words that you and I could share and understand, not in words that we could use to tell or write his story.

Therefore, I have taken it upon myself to try to tell his story, well a bit of his story, for him. Not to tell a story about him, looking at him and making observations from the outside. But to try to tell his story from his perspective, from the inside looking out at the world, experiencing all the stuff that happens to him or goes on around him. To try to tell Harry's story in a way that accounts for and acknowledges his internal thoughts and feelings.

So therefore, I feel I have no choice but to unapologetically talk for him about the experiences he has; and possibly most difficult, I will also try to speak for him about his experiences of being himself. It's not going to be easy; it might not even be right (of course it won't be), but I think Harry deserves his story to be told. I think it is important that other people, people like you, get to know that Harry, and people like Harry are out there, living their lives somewhere amongst us. There are thousands of people, actually tens of thousands of people like Harry living their lives around us, and their numbers are slowly but steadily growing!

Anyway, this is not a big book, so it shouldn't tax you in terms of the effort or the time you will need to read it. And it's not a sad book, so don't go prejudging it and putting yourself off. But I think it would be nice for Harry to share his life with you, and people like you, so that his voice is heard, so that Harry's life is marked in some meaningful way, so that his 'silence' is finally acknowledged.

Harry, and other people like him shouldn't have to remain silent just because other people can't, or can't be bothered, to even try to listen.

Okay Harry, I've been wanting to do this for a while now. So here goes; I hope it does you justice …

Graham

'I want to trip inside your head
Spend the day there
To hear the things you haven't said
And see what you might see'

Opening Lyrics of **U2's 'Miracle Drug'**:

[From the album - *How to Dismantle an Atomic Bomb*]

I can't sleep ...

I can't sleep ... I'm just laying here half-awake, half-asleep, and then half-awake again.

Here I am, half in and half out of being asleep ... in my own little world, in the one world I know, and the only world that has me in it. This is all there is for me, the only world I've ever known, the only reality I've ever been in ... but this is a surprise, having you here, you, here in my world, here in my head, listening to me.

Yes, that's new.

It's a bit strange really, if I'm honest ... but I'm happy to give it a go if you are. I'm happy to share my world with you if you want to hang around in it for a while. It's actually quite nice to have you here, to think that someone is listening, to have someone acknowledge me and my life, my inner reality, my thoughts and feelings. It makes a nice change.

Other people also pop in and out of my world, but not like this. Yes, they do pop in, in and out, now and then, but they never really get inside my world. Not inside of my own lived experience, not fully, not properly, not like me. I'm the only one who lives inside my world, who fully occupies it. I'm the only person who has lived their whole life here.

There are some things in it, in my world, not just the stuff that is happening right now. There are some things that aren't just me in the here and now, the me of and in this moment. There are some things that I've experienced, some stuff that I've done, and some stuff that's been done to me, that also somehow still exists as a part of my world.

It's the invisible field of lived experience, casting a misty shadow that flows in time through the present, through the stuff I do and feel now … but mainly my world is made up of just me, like now, just me, half-awake and half-asleep here in my world, the world that is made up of me and my life's experiences.

It's pretty quiet at the moment … my world is a quiet world just now … and I'm here, just dozing in and out … just quietly, wordlessly, me being me.

I often wake in the night, most nights really, dozing in and out … I'm often asleep in the day as well, dozing in and out … and when I wake, I always seem to wake up into the same world, my world, a world that is both out there and in my head, both at the same time … and that's okay, because my world is familiar, reassuring and familiar. It's the only thing that is … and then I can doze off again, feeling okay that my world is still out there. That it is still mine, still the same, still familiar, still my world.

So yes, I'm Harry … well, I think Harry's my name; it is certainly a kind of distinct sound that I hear around me a lot, although if I'm honest my hearing isn't that good. But it must be something important because it's always being said nearby … not at the moment, but when people are around me. It's Harry this, Harry that, Harry the other, so the really familiar 'Harry' bit must mean something. It must be significant … well it feels significant, significant to me, and reassuring. It feels that this sound is just for me, or about me, so I'm going to claim it as mine.

Anyway, enough about that, about me being called something, about me being called Harry ... and about me having you here in my world ... I'm still not really awake, I'm still not really asleep. I'm still dozing in and out, passing effortlessly between the easy shades of sleep and wakefulness, half in my world ... and half not.

So, actually, this isn't the best time to have chosen to pop into my world. I'm not at my bright and cheery best just now. You'll have to wait a little while before I properly warm up to this task, to show you properly round my world, in my life. Just be patient with me, please ...I think it's going to take us both a little while to get used to this.

Eeeeeaaaahhhhh, ya, yaaa, yaaaaa, eeeeeeeeaaaaahhhh, ya, yaaa, yaaaaa!!!!!!!!!

Oh ... Oh ... Oh no ... Oh no, there she goes again, there she goes, making that racket.

It does my head in, honestly it does; it's the same almost every night. Suddenly, as if out of nowhere, in the middle of the night, shrieking at the top of her voice, and when she starts it goes on and on, over and over, over and over and over again ... first with the "Eeeeeaaaahhhhh"-ing, and then it goes onto all the "ya, yaaa, yaaaaa"-ing ... it's always the same, again and again, on and on, over and over.

Just when I was drifting off, just when I was relaxing back into some lovely sleep ... it's like she knows just when to start ... yes, it's like she knows just the right time to stop me from floating gently back into my all-embracing sleep state again. I'm not being nasty or nothing, but I've had this going on for as long as I can very vaguely remember, and I can only very vaguely remember most things. Suddenly, out of the dark, the screaming and the shrieking, call it what you will, and I've never really got used to it; it still goes right through me, through my whole body, especially when she gets to the final ear-wrenching *"ya, yaaa, yaaaaa"* bit.

It's the same every night. At first it starts real quiet, but then she ... well, then it quickly builds up, louder that is, and longer, and no one can stop her. It starts as a low, drawn-out babbling and jabbering, but then it quickly gets louder ... and then it builds and builds, louder and louder, and for a while it kind of circles around, all confused rhythm and repetition ... but then finally, finally it escalates into its eruption of nerve shattering screeching.

Then she stops, ahhhhhh, just for a short while ... but once that brief pause of calming quietness is done with, it all starts again, over and over, again, the same ... not a single thought for anyone else ... over and over; to its eye-watering extended finishing. And then, after another quiet intake of breath, back she starts again, back at it, just the same as before ... round and round, soft and quiet babblings, then on, louder and louder, faster and faster, building to its nerve-shredding, recurrent finale.

And it's always so much worse when it's dark, like now, when I'm trying to sleep. I suppose it's not her fault really, but it doesn't half get right on my nerves; I'm only human after all … I can only take so much. I just wish she would give it a rest, at night, when I'm trying to sleep … perhaps they could do something, give her something, anything, just to shut her up.

Anyhow, perhaps now that I'm more fully awake I should tell you a bit more about myself. It'll be a nice distraction from that racket. It'll help block that out.

So yes, I am Harry … we've already sort of established that, or at least I think we have. Anyway, it is unlikely that you know me. No, you probably don't know me or indeed anyone else who is really very much like me … most people don't … and I am just guessing that you are one of those 'most' other people.

So yes, it's probably unlikely that you really know someone like me, someone who has apparently managed to learn so very little over such a long period of time, actually over an entire lifetime. It is probably unlikely that you will know someone like me, someone who has had such a really, really, profoundly difficult job in learning … learning just about anything and everything; the things that other people, other walking and talking people (which I'm going to presume includes you – well the talking bit at least), generally just take for granted.

You see, I've been inhabiting this world, my world, for all my life, long past the point that I can remember, but I still haven't learned to talk; not at all, not even a single word. Yes, not a single word in all my life, over all that time; can you believe it? Well, you need to because it's true. As yet, I haven't muttered that momentous, magical first word; not yet, not one … and it's almost certain, yes, really, absolutely, utterly, almost certain, that I never will. Not now.

So yes, it's true, not one single meaningful, recognisable, proper talking, languagey word has ever escaped my lips, not once … not ever in all my life. So, to put it simply for you, that means I don't talk. Not just that, it means that I can't talk; well, not with words.

Not only do I not talk, but it also means that I can't really understand other people's wordy, languagey talk when they talk to me. I can't understand any of the words they use to me, at me, or around me ... that's just how it is, and how it's always been for me. Not one word meaningfully ever exchanged with another human being. Well blow me down (but not literally!).

Now, and I mean no offence by this, but all those words that you and people like you use with each other, well they are a language I don't understand; they, words that is, are things that I can't make any meaning from. No matter how much I have tried (although to be honest, I haven't tried that hard – I couldn't see any point), and how hard others have tried, to get me to understand (and believe me they have tried, and indeed some continue to try to this day) words are just so much wishy-washy noise going on around me, nonsense noises. But those high-pitched screeching noises that the lady of the night (for politeness's sake shall we give her a name? How about Margaret?), makes, well those noises, Margaret's noises, actually make much more sense; well, they do to me.

Yes, Margaret's screeching and shrieking noises make much more sense. I get a feeling from her noises that I can feel, her night-time screeching sounds somehow resonate within me. The sounds, well they play across my body, along my fibres, and on up through my nerves and arrive in my head as readymade feelings. I know she's upset; I know she's afraid; and I know she can't handle it. I can tell all that from the shape of her sounds. She's beyond herself, out of control, utterly pissed off with constantly being upset and afraid, and not being able to handle it. Her sounds must be a kind of release for her; I know it, I can feel it.

I know what her sounds mean, because they make sense to me just as sounds, the rhythm and tone and sharpness, they all come together to all make sense ... they fit with a feeling I can understand ... but words, your kind of wordy language words, words without tone and rhythm and shape, well to me they are just sounds that fall on and off my ears; so many different, meaningless, nonsense noises.

However, not understanding words doesn't stop me from hearing them being said around me all the time; well, just about all the time, when people are around, and at other times as well ... indeed, I'm often placed in my chair in front of a big black box of moving shapes and colours that sends out a constant stream of wordy-type language sounds (when I'm awake and out of bed, as you will find out later, I am usually strapped into some kind of chair). There's one of them big black telly boxes there in the corner of the room. Yes, and I'm often left there, stuck in front of it and its dancing colours, shapes and sounds for long periods of time. I just wish I knew what it was for; what it did, and why.

So, there I will be, stuck in my chair, not watching the blurry shapes of colour move across the telly box (my head usually points up in the wrong direction anyway, and my eyesight isn't great either), not listening to the echoing noisy nonsense noises … it's no wonder so many people just sit and rock themselves away, hour upon hour, or sometimes even hit themselves, on the head or in the face; I know Margaret often does it; although to be fair, not always when the telly box is on.

Actually, being stuck in front of the telly box is just like so much of the stuff I get taken to see or be a presence at. You see, I don't often get that involved in things, no, not properly involved as a part of something (although in all honesty, I can't get properly involved in much). So generally, I just play the part of an outside observer (even with my poor eyesight). Yes, mainly in my life, I'm playing the role of an outsider looking in, or an insider looking out – sometimes I'm not sure which, maybe it's both.

But maybe, when I'm in some of these places, having these 'outside looking in' experiences, perhaps something else is going on, something I'm not aware of. Perhaps there's something going on I can't see or hear, or feel, something going on behind my back … perhaps I'm missing something. Or perhaps I'm there for another reason, perhaps it's about me just being there. Perhaps that's all that counts, all that matters. Perhaps I'm not there to join in, but to represent something, to be a representative of something … perhaps that's what I'm doing, perhaps that's my role, perhaps that's why I'm there. I don't know; how could I?

So often, when I don't know what it is that I'm supposed to be doing, or representing, when I'm in these places, having these experiences, well actually, most of the time, I just switch off. I just switch off from all the stuff around me, all the stuff outside of me. I don't mean to be rude or anything, but I just ignore it all, all the stuff out there, if it doesn't make any sense to me… all the words, all the outside world, all the stuff I'm supposed to watch or experience or be part of … so I let most of it just go by me, just wash over and around me. In my head I'm there, and I'm not there, I'm in my head.

So often I am there, but really, I'm here inside myself, only really present behind my eyes, in my own head, absorbed in doing the few things I can and do actually do; like now, suffering in silence, listening to that racket … yes, Margaret's still at it, screaming and screeching like a good-un. Although generally, most of the time, suffering isn't the right word … being me isn't something I suffer from (not like I think it must be being Margaret), not normally, but it is now, what with Margaret's racket going on, and on, and on.

Actually, that thing about understanding stuff, or more accurately not understanding stuff, stuff like language, well that is something that I suppose sets me and people like me apart from people like you; you who's reading this book. We're usually pretty poor, no actually really, extremely poor at building up our understanding of lots and lots of stuff. Not everything, but most things, things that you, and people like you, just get on with without thinking; things like walking and talking, using words and language, and stuff like that …

Even the most usual, everyday simple stuff … well, that stuff is usually well beyond me and people like me … although actually, I don't think that 'simple' is the right word. This everyday common stuff that people like you think is simple, well that stuff is usually quite or even very complicated. It's just that most people, again, people like you (honestly, I'm not trying to pick on you) … but most people like you take getting to understand the everyday, normal kind of stuff (normal for you that is), for granted. You just learn it as you go along, mostly without even noticing it.

Stuff like what things are, what things do, where things come from, what time of day it is, what things are called, what things are for, how things work, how things go together, what colour things are, using my hands, standing up, saying words, going to the toilet, that kind of stuff … yes, everyday stuff like that. Stuff like what's okay to put in your mouth, and what isn't. Actually, all that everyday kind of stuff is, when you look at it closely (if you can), in real detail (if you can be bothered), it's mostly, most often, really complicated; even if you don't realise it, it is, and it usually takes quite a lot of learning.

Learning those everyday kinds of things will no doubt have been easy for you, and people like you. You'll have learned it all without any effort, mostly without even having to try. You'll have learned a lot of it before you can remember; before you even knew you were you ... but learning that kind of stuff isn't at all easy for me; most of it ranges from the highly difficult and therefore highly unlikely, to the downright impossible - there's just too much processing involved, too much stuff to take in and put together and work out in my head ... too much head work needed for me to understand what I need to understand for me to understand it.

You see, in reality, I don't really know anything that you (yes, okay, and people like you) would see as being proper in the proper way of being proper 'facts' and 'knowledge' ... in the subjective, personal reality of my world, the world I live in and learn in, I know hardly anything about what's going on 'out there', out there in the wider world, in the world shared by other people, people like you. To be honest, I don't really know anything, about anything, outside of my own lived experience. Although I am the world expert on that.

Generally, with that kind of doing and knowing stuff, well I'm not much use, not much use at all ... I'd openly admit it, if only I could. That's just how things are; that's just who I am.

But on the other hand, I am very friendly, I really am, and I'm very reliable. Everyone knows the kinds of things I do, which admittedly isn't much, and how well I always behave. I've never hurt anyone, not deliberately ... I can't really, not physically, not on purpose, but I wouldn't anyway; I'm just not that kind of man. Surely that must play in my favour when people make judgements about me. And I've never told a lie or cheated on anyone ... I've never bullied anyone, and I've never intentionally caused any trouble for anyone, ever, not intentionally ... yes, surely that must count for something?

Sorry, I feel I'm getting a bit ahead of myself here, pushing on a bit too fast ... perhaps it's because I'm still tired, and having you here in my world, listening to me, has taken me by surprise; I certainly wasn't expecting it.

So, as we go along together, to help you, the person now reading this book, the person now here with me, well, I feel I should take this opportunity to try to tell you a bit about myself, in a bit more detail; a bit about who I am, about what happens to me, a bit about what goes on around me, about what I see and what I do, just so that you can understand a bit better about me and my life, just so that you can understand a bit about what it might be like to be me, or someone like me.

But I wouldn't blame you if you put the book down now ... if you just put it to one side and left it there. You probably won't be the first, and anyway it wouldn't matter to me, I wouldn't know: how could I?

Perhaps there is already within you a sense of disbelief: surely no one is really like that? Surely no one is that disabled? Can't walk, can't talk, can't understand almost anything? Not one word, not ever, never ... surely no one is really that bad?

Perhaps you are too busy, perhaps you don't really have the time right now: perhaps you'll pick it up again later ... perhaps? After all, you've got your own life to live, your own difficulties and troubles to cope with, your own worries to consider.

Or perhaps there's been a creeping sense of discomfort, something not quite conscious, but just now pushing through: a feeling that's a bit unwelcome, uninvited; a slight sense of queasiness perhaps, about a person that lacks so much of what normal, everyday people, people like you (yes, there I go again) take as the most basic requirements to be a functioning, adult human being? Not walking, yes, I can get that; in a chair, yes, that's no big deal nowadays ... but not talking, never having said a single word, not one, as an adult; and was there mention of not ever learning to use a toilet, never being continent, neither front nor back, as an adult, never? Come on now, surely not.

No, really though, I wouldn't blame you if you put the book down now. It's probably not relevant to you, is it? It's not really worth your while spending the time and effort ... for what? What else can happen? He can't do anything anyway, so what is the rest of his book going to be about? Nothing presumably ... and it's just made up anyway. Its not even real!

So, please do put the book down now if you feel that way, I wouldn't blame you; it really is okay. I won't actually know anyway, so go on put it down, get a better book instead. Get a proper book: a book that's made up about somebody exciting who does loads of interesting stuff; a book by someone great who says they did a load of great things; a book about someone beautiful to look at or listen to, or something ... just something you can relate to.

I really won't mind, honest. I am used to it, no one listening, people getting out of the way when I come down the street.

So, in that way it's okay. But I will carry on, just in case any of you have bothered to stick with it; perhaps you're the only reader left by now.

Yes, perhaps it's all down to you?

Anyway, reading on might be worth your while, it just might. You might learn something useful; unlikely I know, but it is just possible. So once Margaret has quietened down, I'll see if I can tell you a bit more about myself, about my life, about being me for just one day. I can tell you more about what I can do, as well as what I cannot do, and perhaps you'll come to see me in a new kind of light … possibly; you never know.

Lucky for you it won't take long, because if you get to know about my everyday life, then you will get to know about most of my life; you see it's pretty much the same, day in, day out. That's not a bad return for your efforts; and perhaps, just perhaps, you will actually see me or someone like me about the place. You might feel a bit more confident to come and meet me, to try to say something to me, something that I can sort of understand, something that will be meaningful, meaningful to me anyway … but we can come to that bit later.

Anyway, after all that I'm a bit tired again, actually really tired, what with all this made up talking in my head; I'm not used to it.

So, if you'll just excuse me for a bit, I'll just shut my eyes now and try to ignore Margaret's shrieks and screams … yes, like I always try to do, although it takes a bit of doing. I'll ignore

her … yes that's it, I'll just shut my eyes … I'll just shut my …
I'll just …

My back is aching …

I'm back again, half-awake and half-asleep, like before … but
now I'm not at all comfortable. My back is aching. Somehow,
in my bit of sleep, I've ended up with my arm caught right
underneath me, and my sharp and hard elbow is now sticking
into me, into my side. And what's worse still, no matter what I
do, I can't get it out from under me … I just can't physically
manage it. I'm not strong enough, and I'm not bendy enough,
and I can't get it all together enough to either pull it out or roll
myself off of it.

"Uhh … uhh … uhh … uhh … uuhh … uuuhhhh"

No, I can't …

"Uhh … uhh … uhh … uhh … uuhh … uuuhhhh"

No, no, I still can't …

"Uhh … uhh … uhh … uhh … uuhh … uuuhhhh … uhh …
uuhh … uuuhhhh"

No, no, no, I still can't …

It doesn't help being so weak; it really doesn't. Pound for
pound I'm as weak as they come, so that makes the control
of all my body bits just so difficult, especially as I'm also

physically very stiff, and so that's not a good combination; and sharp, 'stuck-under' elbows are sometimes the result.

Wait though … I think I can hear something, someone coming … perhaps they know, perhaps they can hear me, and they know my 'Uhh … uhh … uhhing' sounds. They know what those sounds might mean.

Yes, that's good … they can turn me, roll me, un-elbow me, and sort out the foamy shapes and pillows that they stick under and around me … wedging me in place, keeping the right bits of me, including my arms and elbows, where they should be, in the right places, mostly.

Yes, told you, here they are, quietly, no nonsense, so as not to disturb, and here they go … a bit of gentle back and forth, rocking gently this way then back again, just enough, don't overdo it, not too much … and yes, that's it; it's out, that's better, much better … I'm back in good shape, each bit back where it should be, back and sorted, and again wedged in on both sides, to keep me all straight and sorted.

Just trying to get comfy with my kind of warped back is something that only a few of you will ever experience or come close to understanding. I reckon most of you won't give your back a first or second thought, well maybe some of you, and you have my sympathy if you do. But my back is off-the-scale all over the place; it twists and curves this way and that, in and out from top to bottom … it's not just really bad, it's really, really, really bad; and as I get older it gets even worse.

Most of the time, when I'm up, I have to be put in my own special, Harry's back shaped chair, which holds me in place and stop me rocking back and forth ... just so that I can sit up a bit sort of straight. Although, when I'm in my chair I am often left tilted really far back, too far back, and therefore facing sort of upwards. So often I end up being positioned looking upwards at ... well not much really, just up towards the top of walls or the ceiling where the shadows lurk, up into that empty dull and silent space; and with my poor eyesight, focusing on nothing really.

Anyway, for now I'm comfy again, and warm, and I can feel myself drifting off again ... feeling warm ... warm and comfy again ... quiet all around... my hard and sharp elbow back where it should be ... eyes heavy, falling shut ...falling asleep.

Who knows, now I might be dreaming ...

Who knows, now I might be dreaming. Yes, perhaps I'm dreaming all of this stuff about me telling you my story, and about you being here in this book with me. Perhaps I'm dreaming it all ... perhaps? Dreaming but hearing and seeing my own inner voice translated into your kind of words ... yes, maybe? I don't know. Perhaps I'm actually awake and all of this is real?

But if I am dreaming, what would I possibly dream about? It's hard to say, of course it is, especially for me. At the best of times, when I am fully with it, fully awake that is, my memory of things is pretty rubbish; no, actually really seriously rubbish. There is generally very little that clearly comes back to me from all the things back there in my past ... and that's when I'm fully awake.

But sometimes, just sometimes, I do get a feeling, yes, a sort of feeling that I have half-pictured or half-sensed something when half-asleep, something not from out there, but from inside here ... something created or recovered from somewhere deep inside of me. A feeling or sense of some things or people I have encountered before ... a dreamily sensed feeling that somehow this thing, whatever it is, feels vaguely familiar; it is somehow of me, even from me, but not in my control ... and although whatever it is maybe started or is related to something somewhere out there, it's also kind of not there, not anywhere. It always feels as if it's just out of reach.

Yes, perhaps I am half-asleep, as I know something is happening ... kind of happening. It feels like I'm drifting around somewhere in-between ... but I sense I am feeling feelings in this half-somewhere place; feelings somehow associated with someone or something that was once familiar to me. But I can't tell what it is, or who they are, and so I can't tell you. Not even here.

But anyway, when I do come fully around, when I am properly awake, I can't remember any of these dreams. I don't really, properly remember things anyway, not really in any detail, not with any understandable understanding, not in a clear way like you might. So remembering dreamy half-sensed feelings of something out there, in here but out of reach, is always going to be a bit of a stretch; especially for me.

But who knows, perhaps when I'm really fully, deeply asleep, perhaps then I do dream. Perhaps then I clearly dream, and have really meaningful dreams, meaningful to me that is. But perhaps then the memory of my dream just fades away out of mind and sight as I start to wake up. Perhaps my nights are filled with wonderful dreams, of wonderful times, with wonderful people, and I can't remember any of it, not even that I've dreamed it. Perhaps it is all wiped away in a flash as I come round and arrive into wakefulness, everything instantly and utterly wiped from my weak and feeble memory … what an absolute bummer that would be!

Perhaps I'm being a bit unfair to my memory. It isn't as if there is nothing there, nothing at all. It doesn't mean I can't remember anything, any impressions of things. But there isn't any detail. I actually do keep some of the impressions that things have had on me up there in my memory banks: the impressions some things leave on my senses; the impressions some things leave on my feelings; even the impressions some things have on my feelings about myself.

The difficult thing for me is that I can't bring these general impressions together to form any clear and recognisably conscious word-like thoughts. So, I can't describe these impressions, unfortunately not even to myself. But I can feel them, I can kind of know of them without being able to know really what they are. I know they are there, but I can't tell myself what they are really, properly about, or what they really, properly mean … but perhaps we're not that different there, you and I, maybe that's not that uncommon.

But it's not just the remembering of stuff from back in the murky and distant past that's difficult. No, for me it's the whole thing. In fact, it's difficult for me to get stuff in there, into my memory, in the first place; even stuff that's happening now. So, that really makes a lot of this remembering and understanding, and understanding and remembering, really very difficult for me; they kind of go together, or in my case they don't.

Because I can't hold hardly any bits of stuff in my mind at any one time, there at the front of my mind, I really struggle to link anything or any things together, to build up something of more than one thing at any one time. Therefore, that makes it really hard for me to learn anything that you might call learning from them, from these, my experiences; well, certainly not much that I am clearly aware of.

For simplicity's sake, and I like a lot of simplicity, if I can't hold more than one thing in my mind at any one time, then obviously I am going to really struggle to bring more than one thing together, to link anything to other things not happening at the same time. So, I really struggle, and most often fail, to go on and draw together any clear or general thoughts or clear feelings about my encountered experiences. It generally just doesn't happen for me, it doesn't sink in; not in the way it does for you, automatically, without trying. It means that unless an experience is something I have done many, many times (and is simple, with very few things or bits to it), then any such an experience is going to seem entirely new or utterly confusing to me.

So, it's really hard, and it takes ages, and many, many repeated goes to slowly build up my general knowing about things, even about the kinds of stuff that I already know a bit about, the things that are really familiar to me; the things most often present in my world. But I do need these things, these things that I know a bit about and am very familiar with, I need them to be very much the same as each time before, so that I can feel I understand them, so that I can know what they are about, and what they do and what perhaps they are going to lead on to.

But saying that, I can learn some things, of course I can, and I do. Yes, I can build up my thoughts and feelings about a few things. But again, I do need these things to be really, or at least very nearly the same as the things I already know about. I need newish things to be similar to things that have gone before, but not quite exactly the same, so that I can then very slowly build up some slightly new impressions of these things and thus slightly (ever so slightly, and ever so slowly) expand my current thoughts and feelings on a few (very slightly less familiar) things. When this does happen for me, I am just doing it, unaware that it's going on, but none-the-less learning something very slowly when it takes place. So perhaps we're not that different; perhaps it's just the size of the task and the speed at which things happen that's so very different. Yes, maybe that's not too different at all?

But the language thing – well understanding any of that has evaded me. It's too complex for me to link up those kinds of unreal and unfamiliar wordy things to other things that are real and bear no resemblance to the wordy things used to

27

somehow label them with. And it all goes by in a flash …
Crikey, no wonder I can't do it! But moving on …back to my
dreaming.

Perhaps it is these simple impressions and slightly, ever so
slightly expanded ideas from the day before that come back
to me and swirl around in my head as I dream. Perhaps these
impressions and ideas slowly move around in my head, trying
to find the right place to settle, to find a resting place that helps
me, just a bit, to have new and improved thoughts and
feelings the next day; thoughts and feelings that might stop
with me for a while longer than the brief moments I first
encountered them. Perhaps these impressions and ideas
tease out a tiny bit of new ground in my head, in what I know,
reassuring me that the things I do know still make some
sense; and possibly, just occasionally, they might just add a
little bit more of something onto my old impressions and ideas.
Yes, perhaps.

But also, you see, there is a difference. There's a difference
between that fleeting moment of remembering something, of
just reconnecting with a resurfacing old and familiar
impression or thought, there is a difference between that and
actually learning to understand something a bit better; having
bigger and better impressions and thoughts … and that can
only happen for me when something has happened often
enough to make it stick. It needs to happen to me quite often
so that it can finally find its place and settle down somewhere
in my head … that's when it might finally move across from
one place to another, changing in my head from a brief
memory of an actual, single thing into a more solid sort of

understanding of that and other similar things. Blimey, it's complicated isn't it! No wonder it's so hard for me.

Although it might be interesting to think about which comes first, the memory then the understanding, or the understanding and then the memory. Which one? I can't imagine being able to remember stuff that I don't already know something about, that I don't already understand in some way. And equally I am not going to be able to understand something that I have not yet built up some memory of.

It all feels a bit of a circle round that doesn't connect up for me, what with all the stuff that I don't remember and therefore don't understand or recognize as meaningful. And all the stuff I don't understand and therefore don't recognise and therefore can't lay down any memories about. I'm not sure where to go with all that. So yes, I need to remember stuff to understand it, but I also need to understand stuff to recognise and then remember it … but which comes first? I don't know, of course I don't. You'll just have to figure that bit out for yourself.

Anyway, it's still very late or very early, and I am still very tired … and this stuff is getting way, way too complicated for me. To be honest it's been like that from the start. Perhaps I was just dreaming that last bit, the bit just then about the dreaming, and the remembering, and the understanding, and the recognising, and the remembering, or not in my case… and if I was, then that would be nice. Yes, it would be nice to be able to dream complicated things like that.

Yes, and as I said before, perhaps my nights are really filled with wonderful dreams, of wonderful times, with wonderful people sharing wonderful experiences, and then as I wake it all disappears off in the first flicker of the eye, maybe that's what happens. Perhaps I'm at my most alive, my most active, my most profound, when I'm dreaming, and then, with a blink of my waking eyes, it all just disappears, all that wonderful stuff, with wonderful people … what a pisser that would be … it'd be just my luck!

Let's see then, am I dreaming? Could I tell anyway?

It's so quiet, so peaceful, so dreamy. So perhaps I am half-awake and half-asleep. Perhaps it can be a bit of both, not fully one thing nor fully the other … time going by, slowly, slowly… where does it come from, that time stuff, and where does it go once we're done using it?

Actually, no, I am still awake, just; even now, even at this time. Although, to be honest, I never really know what time it is, not properly. I can tell if it is dark or if it is light, or if I am fully awake, when I am really, fully awake, but not much more than that. I know when I am hungry, I suppose, when it should be time to have something, or when it's time to move if I have been sitting still for too long or lying in the same position past the time it remains comfortable … so I know something about time.

But I can't really put it together into a proper sort of time, not your sort of time of the day type of thing … but actually, I don't really need to, other people do that for me, so I'm not too bothered. I don't miss something I've never had, so I'm honestly not at all fussed. Although in a different sense, I don't miss it because I have plenty of it. So yes, I do have time, plenty of time, I just don't need to go over the top with thinking about it or naming it. I don't go getting all worried about what time it is now, or what time it will be soon or what I should call it. I can leave that to others, the other people who need to know about it. They'll sort that out for me ... if they have the time.

But I do know about and recognise some familiar bits or patterns or orders of time, and the time shape of really very familiar activity, like if someone puts me to bed, or if I am being hoisted into the bath, or when I am in the kitchen. Then I do kind of know what time it is generally, in a lived sense, and what is coming up next. I can put together those patterns or sequences of activity that are very, very familiar to me, across my life, and that is probably more than some people can do. But I can't put it all together; not the whole this starts now, then this happens, then another thing happens next, then something else, and so on and so on, and then it gets dark. That level of knowing time, what happens in five or six steps time; well, that is still a bit beyond me.

What I need are some easily recognisable starting signals, some familiar thing, some familiar part of an activity, at the start, to start it all off; then I kind of know about time, in a way, in a sensed and familiar way ... in the sense that I can recognise a particular familiar thing as happening now, so this is now ... and then this equally familiar other thing comes next; yes I get that. When I have been through this simple and predictable ordering of things many, many times before, one familiar thing first, then another, and then other familiar things to follow … that's the kind of time that I know, not the other sort, not the named type of time that others seem to need.

But I'm fine with that, I'll leave that other sort of time to others, that'll suit me fine … but still, really, where does it come from? And where does it go to once we've used it? I don't know. Do you?

'I want to hear you when you call
Do you feel anything at all
I want to see your thoughts take shape
and walk right out'

(U2: Miracle Drug)

Dreaming … dreaming …

Dreaming ... dreaming … no, honestly, I am this time. This time I am definitely asleep, trust me, and I really am dreaming (yes, I know this is difficult and it seems a bit contrived, but you'll just have to go with it. Please, for my sake).

Shadowy shapes and shades are gently placing themselves in place, in amongst themselves … just traces really, traces of colours and shapes. Shapes like objects but not objects, shapes like shapes but not shapes, shapes like, well, mere wisps of somethings or somebodies. At times it's as if I can see them from all their sides, from all the angles, from just one place, from behind my eyes, all at once, but still not make them out … and they are moving, in and amongst themselves, forming and reforming, merging and emerging all at the same time.

And, and, and there's an old familiar sense of something that wafts out from amongst the shapes. It might even be the shape of a smell (and it's not me). I don't like it; it smells dark, it smells sickly sweet, and it comes and goes, like someone slowly breathing at me, on me, right up into my face. It seems to be a smell that has colours and a shape mixed up with it, and bits of feelings in there as well ... and none of it is clear, or clearly what it is or is supposed to be. I feel uncertain; not scared, but not sure what's going on, what's going to happen next, unable to understand or control what's going on … just like I often feel when I'm awake!

It's like half an impression of something or a feeling of something: not quite what it is, having bits of it almost there and almost not. There's not enough to make any real sense of, to get a proper hold of, for me to understand. It is all just nearly there, nearly kind of forming, kind of familiar, but not, and then going back again, leaving faint impressions of a moment, a smell, a shape, a colour, maybe even the outlines of face, there for a moment, and then gone; and I don't like it. I don't like not knowing what or who it might have been … and what it wants from me now. Again, I don't like that feeling, out of control, just like I often feel when I'm awake!

It's a shame that there are no wonderful times, doing wonderful things with wonderful people. That's a pity that is.

Then it goes, all of it, in the flicker of an eye as my half-awake mind shifts its gears and slowly pulls me away from my sleeping dreaming self, pulling me out towards the real world … half-in and half-out, but not fully either. That's where I often feel I am, somewhere in between. Sometimes I'm more out and with it, and sometimes less so; sometimes both a bit out and a bit in, and not really knowing which.

Perhaps it's hard for you to imagine being like that, being like me … never with clear and proper thoughts, not being able to explain stuff to myself, like my dreams. Not like you can, not like you can think openly about things, or think you can. Not being able to tell yourself who you are and what you are doing, not being able to freely look out onto the real world, knowing it, feeling it, knowing that you are feeling it, knowing that you are knowing it, being free to be self-aware, maybe even when you're dreaming.

Yes, I suppose it must be hard to image being someone like me, someone who doesn't think with words, someone who can't even imagine that words can have meanings other than being just emotional noises, someone without an inner voice of words and thoughts that is there to remind them of who they are, and of their own existence. Maybe you're wondering how can someone without an inner voice, without a voice to voice their inner private thoughts ever be conscious in the same sense as you? How can they be aware of themselves as themselves, and of their own activity and existence in the world? Well, take it from me, they can be, and they are … I am, therefore, well, I am.

Perhaps you think that that is what makes us humans different, different from all other things around us; that ability to talk and be fully aware of ourselves and have thoughts about and a conscious awareness of ourselves. And there I am without a single word in my head … vacant, empty of words, empty of describable thoughts, silent except for my sounds, my wordless sounds, with nothing clearly meaning anything … just feelings and senses and impressions in my head swirling around.

But yes I do feel, and yes, I do sense, and although I may not have any wordy language thoughts in my head because of my profound difficulties in learning new things, especially words, I do have many sensed feelings of, and impressions about the world, my experienced world, and my wordless presence in it: so therefore, yes, I am conscious of myself and my world, even if I can't tell other people about it – I just sense it, I feel it and I know it! So, now you know as well: get used to it!

But if you don't mind, you can just relax for a while as I go back to enjoying my dreamlike unconsciousness, whether I'm really dreaming or not. I'm shutting everything down for a while now, until the next time I feel like opening up to the outside world.

The light is just starting to come ...

The light is just starting to come, just pushing in around the edges of the windows, grey and cold and just about see-able. Actually, just on the edge of see-able at the moment, especially if you don't look straight at it, although I have to look straight at it otherwise I can't see it ... and the daytime, light-time noises from outside are just starting to come; not all the time, just now and again, just starting to push away the quiet and the calm ... but my eyes are still feel heavy, and sticky with last night's tiredness.

I'm not really ready yet, not ready to be wide awake, and there's nothing really going on. So off I go again, letting go, relaxing, listening a bit for anything happening, but just being nice and relaxed ... restful ... comfortable ... quiet.

Oh, no, Margaret's started again, and it's not just the noise of her screams and screeching, not this time. I can hear her banging, banging herself, banging herself in the face, hard, right in the face ... that's what she does, hit herself, really hard, and you can't begin to imagine why. Well at times perhaps you can imagine why, if you try to see things with her blank and sightless eyes: she's never been happy, and no-one has worked out why ... she can't tell anyone, whatever it is she has had to bear, and bear it all alone, she has had to

37

keep it inside of herself and find some way of dealing with it, whatever it is ... and this is what she does. This is what she's always done.

Bang, bang, bang. Screech, screech, screech; it's hard enough to hear on the outside, it must be unbearable on the inside, and yet I suppose she just does. So, she keeps on doing it, and doing it to herself. Bang, bang, bang. What must it be like?

Actually, I think I get a bit of the same kinds of feeling sometimes, sometimes when I have to sit in the same place for ages, outside of time, with nothing going on, doing nothing, being nothing, going nowhere, just sitting there, just sitting ... then I think I might be tempted myself, to hit or poke or scratch myself, to do something, to change something, to mark time or to make something happen or someone come; if only I could move my hands and arms enough.

For the first bit of time the helplessness and boredom might seem tolerable, maybe even relaxing ... but then, after a time, the same crushing sameness of it all would set in. And then, with the added weight of time when it seems like forever, followed by the unendurable frustration of not being able to do anything about it: being trapped, and knowing that you can't do anything about it, knowing that you are trapped ... the world not giving you anything that helps, no one giving you anything that relieves the pressure, there being nothing there as a release as you get to, and then beyond the tipping point - the only person you can do anything to is you, the only person you can take something out on is yourself ... and perhaps the rest just follows ... perhaps you end up having no choice in the matter ... perhaps that is better than the alternative.

Perhaps then it just becomes a habit: the first thing you go to as soon as it starts. Perhaps that's where Margaret is now. Perhaps. I have habits, perhaps we all do. Some habits might make sense but there are plenty of others that don't; others that we do because, well, they are a habit, not because we want to, not because it's a good thing, but because we just do it, the habit thing ... and perhaps the hitting is just a habit now. Perhaps it wasn't at the start: perhaps she did it for a good reason at the start, whenever that was, but perhaps now she just does it because she does it ... perhaps she does it out of habit ... or perhaps she does it because she can't not; perhaps she just needs something, something that she can do, rather than endlessly suffer a totally consuming absence of everything.

Perhaps having nothing is the worst thing: perhaps the absence of any sensation is more uncomfortable than the physical sensation of hitting yourself. Perhaps it would cause her more anxiety if the familiarity and dependability of it stopped ... bang-bang-bang, on the face, there it is, I can feel it, I can do it, there again, I can feel it, and I know I can do it. If it stops, then what ... nothing ... emptiness ... still nothing ... something needs to happen, something needs to happen soon ... the uneasiness is starting to rise again, I need a fix for it. I need diverting from myself and the emptiness that hangs too heavy. It's becoming intolerable ... empty ... alone ... nothingness ... so off we go again ... bang-bang-bang, in the face, reassurance, there it is, reassurance - that's me doing that, reassurance and the removal of an intolerable emptiness.

I know what I'm doing, I'm doing what I know. I can feel it and I know who's doing it, its familiarity reminds me of me, its familiarity reminds me of who I am and who I have always been … perhaps that's what she does it for ... but I really don't know; how could I? But I do have a vague feeling about perhaps knowing why. Just a bit.

She obviously can't help it, she can't help herself: it's the hitting that has the upper hand, it's the behaviour that controls her more than her controlling the behaviour ... and she can't tell anyone why she does it: she won't know herself, not knowingly, not in her head. She will just feel the need and then give way to it because it will be so strong, the urge will be forcing her hand, and her own will … her own mind will not have any part to play, her own will will be left on the side-lines as a mere bystander of her own actions. That's sad, and I feel sad when I hear her, even when I'm irritated by it and by her.

And I'll be stuck here having to listen to it … although I think that she is slowing down, getting less driven, less anxious as the light comes on. And I can hear someone moving about: there's a voice, a nice soft voice, a calming voice, nice calm sounds out there where Margaret is, and it seems to be having some effect. Margaret's noise is getting less, the nice soft voice is reassuring, quietening, calming ... oh, I do hope so.

Right, here we go, I'm waking up …

Right, here we go, I'm waking up … waking up to the real world, my real world … waking up properly this time. I can feel it in my body, in my bones. My body has a bit more energy in it; it feels like there is less sleep still in me. The real deep sleepiness is starting to fade, finally ebbing away, gradually leaving a bit more wakefulness in its place.

As the light builds, my world starts to feel more properly here and there around me. It feels as if it is starting to bring itself back up, coming back together around me, piece by careful piece, gently arranging itself into its proper order, with the light bringing itself back into the right kind of day-shapes, shapes that are there for me, shapes that I can recognise.

I'm coming around properly now, my eyes edging bit by bit wider, getting to be more and more open: although I do struggle a bit to control them; my eyes that is. At the best of times my eyes tend to dash around the place a bit, often dancing up and down, flicking on and off things as I try to focus in on whatever it is … and focusing in on stuff isn't always easy due to my positioning, what with the way I sit facing upwards at a slight angle when I'm in my chair. And here in my bed, I can only look out to one side, my usual side, due to my body shape and how I'm wedged in. But if things are up close, then I can focus in on them, for a short while.

But now I'm just trying to look out and across, out from my bed to check that the familiar morning things that should be there are there, that the familiar things are in their proper places, as they should be, as the light moves in to reveal them. It's nice when they are.

You see, when it gets light, I like things to be as I expect them ... if any things I have come to know disappear, then I tend not to know where they have gone; whether they might sometime be coming back, or really even whether they continue to still exist or not. In fact, if things are put out of sight, they do kind of cease to exist for me, unless I am really, really familiar with them. So that's why I like the familiar, the known, the predictable, the regular, the how it should be. I can control it better in my mind, I can to some degree hold it, and retain it and kind of understand it when I have seen it and known many, many times over. Then I can know things that are in the right place at the right time.

But anyway, this morning it all seems okay. I'm looking around as best I can, and things seem to be where they should be, still there in their right and proper places. With the light at the end of the room now really pushing in from around the curtains, I can start to properly sense it all: my bedtime wedges, and the cushions, the bars, they're where they should be. The bed cover, and my body below it; there okay as well. The shapes on the walls, the various blurry large and looming things around the side of my room, yes, they're all still there.

Yes, they seem to be okay, all the things. They seem to be in their right place, all around me, reassuring me with their presence, getting on silently with their own stuff, doing what they are supposed to be doing, not bothering me. In their proper place, here to greet me in the morning. So, how are things? How are things this morning? The things are okay, and therefore so am I.

Although I like them to be around, and I find their presence somehow reassuring, I don't spend much time doing things with them; well, no time at all really. Other people do stuff with them, open them up, put stuff in them, fetch stuff out of them, make strange non-word noises as they bend down and put their heads in them. But actually, most of these things don't really do much for me, or with me.

If I'm honest, I don't really know what these things are for, what they are there to do. Some things do some stuff; like the big telly box in the corner, that makes the noises and has the shapes and lights coming out. Some things have bits that move in and out, or up and down; others just stand there ... they just seem to be happy to be there, doing whatever it is that they are doing, quietly getting on with it, not making a fuss. I can't control them; they don't respond to me ... mostly they don't move when I try to look at them, and they don't turn to try to look at me when I make a noise. They remain separate, aloof really you might say, insensible of me and a mystery to me, staying just there, there in their place, doing what they do, which is a good thing I suppose; for them anyway.

Don't get me wrong, I like it that way, with the familiar arrangement of all these familiar things, I know where I am with them. But perhaps just sometimes you'd think that these things might, just might seem a little bit interested, interested in me, just now and then, just a bit; but I suppose that's 'things' for you. I suppose they're busy being themselves, and have no time left over for me – but that's a bit too self-involved for my liking. So, I suppose I prefer those things I know as people, they're different, they do stuff, they move about, they make interesting noises and some of them sometimes seem interested in me, not like these things now here around me.

Perhaps some things are better than these stay where they and do nothing for me things. Perhaps some things have a nicer side to them. Perhaps there are things out there that do care, that do respond, that are bothered, but I haven't met many of them, not yet. That's not fair actually; there's my bed and my chair, they know me and seem to like being with me, and they certainly do stuff for me. But you never know, perhaps they are like people in the way that they aren't all the same. Perhaps some things are a better class of thing, perhaps more caring, more willing to do stuff, perhaps. Who knows? Not me ... and probably not these things either. Even if some of them did know, I bet they wouldn't tell me, I bet they would keep it to themselves and not let on. Well two can play at that game; I don't do anything for them either. I generally ignore them, these bigger useless things, not give them a second thought (except now, when I'm explaining things to you!).

Although if I'm honest, sometimes I just feel that some of them might be looking, just sometimes. I feel it rather than see it, I just get a sense that something might be looking at me ... but I've never yet caught any of them. But that doesn't mean that some of them don't look sometimes, just occasionally, and perhaps one day I will catch one of them looking, just once, when they least expect it.

And so, time passes, with me laying here: time coming, time going, loads and loads of it, lots of time moving on, passing over me, carrying me slowly forward into the morning. At the moment I don't mind, each bit of time seemingly moves past me weighing nothing, and yet ... and yet, like I've already said, sometimes it can press in on me, when I've had too much pure time undiluted by anything else. The it can press down quite heavily on me, not all the time, just sometimes, pressing down on me from the outside, tightening me up on the inside ... but not now, I'm quite happy to be here waiting for someone to come in, waiting for someone to come and do something to me, waiting for someone to start the day with me.

And this is how it is, at this time, every time at this time. That's what happens, and it's okay ... it's familiar, it comes around, and it keeps coming around, and yes, that's okay, that's what I rely on. Another morning, another familiar time inside my room. Again and again, it comes around, and I am here at this time, with time passing quietly by, inside and outside, and that's nice, time passing by easily, weightlessly ... and today I am okay waiting, for the moment, for a while. Always the same these mornings. And they will come, yes, they always do. I can rely on them; I have to, I have no choice.

Anyway, while we're waiting, perhaps you'd like to know a bit more about me. Perhaps you are wondering what I look like? Perhaps you are wondering if you could recognise me if you saw me on the street? Remember, first impressions count for

45

everything, well a lot anyway, and looks are the first thing that give us that first impression, aren't they?

Although giving you a description of my physical outside won't help you much in getting to know the real me, the person that I really am here, on the inside. Looking at me from the outside will never give you a sense of who I am, of how I tick away inside, of how I get on with being Harry ... well not unless you really looked at me, and looked at me for a long time, and looked at me for a long time in lots of different ways and in lots of different situations. Then you might start to get an idea, seeing me with people, with the people around me, the ones who really know me, then you might get an inkling. A short look at my outside really won't do; a short look at my outside will make you think that I'm utterly useless, and other words might come into your mind to describe how I look. But I'm not useless, and I'm not those other things you thought of, no, not really. Not at all really.

Interestingly, well interesting to me anyway because this is about me, but some people won't look at me at all, not at all; they're frightened to look. They ignore me or pretend not to see me. Or they will look away rather than at the outside part of me. Perhaps I shouldn't blame them ... perhaps they can't deal with the feelings they feel at the idea of my different body shape, what with all its tight twists and sharp angles, so different to their own outsides. Perhaps they are just not able to deal with their own thoughts or feelings about how I came to look and be who I am. Maybe it's their own feelings that get in their way; perhaps that's the problem, their problem, their feelings.

Whilst there are others, usually the littler louder ones, the ones who excitedly run around when I'm out somewhere. Well often when they get close to me, then they will just stop, stop still, and then look, really look, really look straight and hard at me. Sometimes they seem unable to take their eyes off of me, until they are dragged away by someone bigger; but still they look back at me, until they disappear somewhere round a corner. But I don't sense that they're being unfriendly; I'd say, more interested, perhaps more wanting to know more, more about me. I hope so, because I quite like the outside look of them, and the nice, excited sounds they make. No, I wouldn't mind having some of them around me more often.

But anyway, when I'm up out of bed, and not in the bath, or on the floor with my wedges and cushions tucked under me, well then you will find me in my chair, in my own Harry's chair. If you do ever see me around, out and about, then you will almost certainly see me in my chair, with someone behind me pushing me wherever I am going. This chair is just for me, and the part that goes under me fits me tightly, cupping me all around my various curves, fitting the various twists and turns of my back and upper body.

Oh, and my hands and arms are also twisted, pulled back really tight into my body; they can barely move at all. And my legs, well to be honest, my legs are so thin and withered that knobbly doesn't really do them justice. They are so thin that they can't support me; nowhere near. So, I don't use them much, just for a bit to kick out when I get excited. So, there's no chance of me ever standing, never mind walking; never was. So, if you do see me out and about, then I will be in my

47

chair, Harry's chair, being pushed around by someone else, standing or walking behind me, doing all the leg work for me. Luckily, they seem to know where they're going, as I generally don't.

However, on the plus side, I'd like to think that facially I carry a certain distinguished air. Perhaps it's something to do with the backward incline of my head, with my taut features and strong jawline raised at an almost aloof angle. And what, with my high and sharp cheek bones, and if I'm in the mood, my winning smile, well I think that should be a real head-turner ... for the right reasons, I hope!

But I do look different to everybody else; I'm one of a kind. Although actually I'm not, not really. I look quite a bit like some other people, people who have profound levels of physical disabilities, or physical deformities as you might say. But that is me, and that is how I look... because, well, I am just such a person. I do have profound and multiple physical disabilities; my body is profoundly misshapen across its entirety when compared to most other people; there really is no getting away from it. That is how it is, and that is how I am. That is who I am. It is how I've always been. But I am still Harry, in my chair, a man of a certain age with a distinguished air about him if you look close enough for long enough.

There are other people who like me carry this label of 'profound and multiple learning difficulties' around with them. But like everyone else, in our own ways we are all different, all still unique, all still individuals ... although obviously we do also have some things in common. We do all share some common characteristics, and it is these characteristics that define us all as members of 'our' group, our 'gang', 'people with profound and multiple learning difficulties'. So, we all have more than one thing that is really, seriously, profoundly disabling, and difficult for us, both in our minds and with our bodies. Yes, profoundly disabled, or profoundly impaired, or really, truly very, very different; whatever or whichever you prefer, that's me, that's us. That's the main thing or things that sets us apart, or as a group brings us together, depending on which side of the divide you sit on.

The major thing that we all share in our group, is that our thinking and understanding and remembering is profoundly restricted to the point that no matter how long we live, and how old we get, we will never get to understand of the kinds of stuff the rest of you take for granted, especially the really tricky and complicated stuff like words and language. But that doesn't mean that people like me, people like us, don't know things, or don't have a view on things. But it does mean that we see and experience the world in very different ways from you and all the other people who don't suffer our kind of really profound difficulties; if suffer is the right word, which I don't think it necessarily always is.

And it's not just the difficulties in thinking and understanding and remembering or the obvious physical stuff with our bodies either. People like me often have other stuff going on or going wrong as well. Many of us, including me, have trouble seeing, and some can't see at all (even if their eyes work okay, some people still can't see because of some bits of damage in a particular part of their brains).

49

I can only see things that are there right there in front of me, right where I'm looking, and I can't really see things so much around at the sides. Also, I can't see things that are too far away, not at all clearly. The further away, and actually not that far away, the more blurred things get, and that's particularly unfortunate for me, because of the shape of my chair, because it has to support the weight of my head for me, I tend to face quite a bit upwards. So, unless someone or something comes right into the space just in front of me, and quite close in, then they remain at best just a blur, and worst invisible (to me that is).

But I suppose in some ways I'm lucky. Some of the people, like Margaret, are completely blind … although she did that to herself, bashing in and scarring up her eyes with all that face-whacking bang-bang-banging stuff. Banged beyond use, banged until only the white parts remain.

Some other people like me may not be too good at hearing either, or they may even be properly, profoundly deaf. Or they may have partial hearing that is also really sensitive as well. They may hear some sounds much more sharply, much more keenly than others, so that some sounds may pass them by completely whilst other sounds, even some apparently quiet sounds, will make them jump with the shock; it's a right mixed bag this multiple impairment stuff, although it's certainly not a lucky dip kind of mixed bag; quite the opposite. Some people are blind and deaf together, both at the same time, to some degree or entirely. That can't be easy; that can't be good.

As if that wasn't enough, some people can find certain kinds of touch extremely unpleasant or un-nerving, being touched by other people can feel really scary and unpleasant. Not always, and not everywhere, but perhaps on their hands or on certain parts of their body; being really uneasy or anxious with certain kinds of touch. They find that really hard, some of them (sorry, for some of us – although luckily, I'm just very ticklish).

Like I've told you about myself already, many of us also have twisted bodies, or oddly shaped physical features. Sometimes it is not just our bodies, but our heads or faces, or we might have crooked, misaligned or even missing legs or arms. Mostly such people, sorry again, we can't walk on our own, and so we have to sit in special chairs and need other people to move us around or physically position us, feed us and toilet us. Yes, that is us, that's me and that's people like me; that's our gang, that's my gang.

But getting back to the important stuff (me that is), it is important that you know that, despite all these things, all these profound difficulties and disabilities, within me, I am me. It's who I am, in fact it's these things that have made me, and still make me who I am; it's all I've ever been. And so, I encounter and experience the world as Harry, day in day out as the man that I am, and all the feelings, and all the thoughts of sorts that I have, come from there; come from me being me.

So yes, on the outside very different, and on the inside I'm also very different in some ways too. Although I don't have any recognizable words, none like yours that you can use as a tool for thinking in your head, I do have feelings, real feelings, just like everyone else. I know and sense happiness, joy, fear, sadness, funness (is that an emotion, it certainly feels like one), the whole range … well perhaps not the whole range, but quite a good range, the simple and straightforward ones anyway. The easily recognised ones.

Although sometimes I can also feel a bit of what you might call shyness. Perhaps that's a bit more of a complicated one, but I do feel something wanting to pull me back or away when I'm in the company of people I don't know, and it's not fear or anxiety. It's something else harder to describe or put an emotional finger on. But also, sometimes, just sometimes, I can even feel a tiny tinge of what you would call jealousy. Yes, I can be jealous of other people, not of who they are, or what they have or can do, but I can at times be just a bit jealous when other people get attention when it's available and not given to me. That makes me feel something, yes, a bit jealous you might say; and it's not nice.

Perhaps there are other emotions that you might have that I don't. Perhaps we have to somehow learn some of our more complicated emotions through experience; perhaps some of the more complicated ones are passed onto us from others? Perhaps some of these emotions are beyond me anyway? Perhaps they are just too complicated for my mind to get involved with? If I knew about these things, I could probably tell you that I don't tend to feel embarrassed, and I certainly don't feel shame. That's an emotion I don't seem to have developed, or learned, or had within me from the start. Although to be honest I don't think it's an emotion I would find particularly useful as I don't think I do anything to be ashamed of, but perhaps that's beside the point.

Also, if I knew what it felt like I would say that I don't feel ambitious, to get or achieve things. Yes, ambition is another emotion, if it is an emotion, which has failed to develop within me. I don't feel an internal drive to achieve specific outside kinds of things, and similarly I am not troubled by feelings of failure, of not becoming the person that I might have dreamt I could become (if I could dream stuff like that – but we've kind of been through that dreaming issue already, haven't we?). I do get frustrated at certain times, at certain things, which is something I can and do feel, but I don't endlessly compare myself with other people around me and feel bad about it.

I'm certainly not a person who strives to get things, physical material things (again I'm not sure that is an emotion). I'm not one for going out and getting stuff, it simply doesn't interest me; although that doesn't stop me from regularly being pushed around the local big place loaded to the roof with all kinds of stuff … being pushed past place after place after place, places full of stuff, and yet more stuff. What can it all be for? I don't know, and I really do not care.

Getting back to the point though, me that is. None of this means that I, as someone with all my profound disabilities and related difficulties, suffer because of my condition; that I suffer in a way that is more profound because of my profound impairments. No, no, not at all. That isn't what I do; suffer from being me, from being Harry.

Although I do have most of the already mentioned difficulties and disabilities, and I can hardly do anything independently for myself, that doesn't make me miserable. No, not a bit of it. Well, actually I will admit that I do gripe on occasions, mainly due to my difficult digestive system (oh, that's another associated condition … I should have mentioned that as well. It's the lack of physical movement you see, the bowel becomes weak and lazy, and then it struggles to move the necessary matter through to the endpoint. But that's another story, and not a very pleasant one). But generally, mostly, I'm not one to moan, as all the people who know me would tell you. You see, it isn't in my character to do so. No, I don't suffer from being me, from being Harry, not at all.

I mean, I could moan. I've certainly got more than enough to moan about if I wanted to, but generally I don't. I'm really quite a cheery chap, because that's my character, that is who I am. That is Harry. No matter how profoundly impaired or disabled I, or anyone else might be, we are all individuals, we all have our own character. Just like everyone else, we are who we are, we are who we have become. Personally, I am and always have been, generally a positive and cheerful person, especially so when I have other positive and cheerful people around me, even more especially when we are enjoying being positive and cheerful together. That isn't particularly surprising, is it? I bet you're probably a bit the same. Perhaps we aren't so different after all?

Although admittedly not everyone like me is, well, like me. Take Margaret, well she suffers (a lot), and does complain (a lot), and at times she makes the rest of us suffer too. She's not as bad as she used to be, but at her worst she just screams and screams, on and on and on she goes; unhappy doesn't come close to covering it.

But actually, even she isn't as bad as she used to be. Often, no, sometimes, she's quite a bit better, but on those other occasions she can still make that racket that shakes my foundations. And she still whacks herself, absolutely whacks herself, full in the face, making her face red and her ears bleed … but like I say, she's not as bad as she used to be; they don't have to use the jacket with a leather belt to stop her.

As I said before, she actually blinded herself with all that hitting, all that bang-bang-banging, hitting herself in the face and eyes. It makes you wonder what she must have been thinking. Well, I suppose she wasn't actually 'thinking', she was just doing it, that behaviour, for whatever reason, but there you go: as they say, there's none as strange as folk.

That thing about thinking and thoughts … it's tricky, because Margaret probably doesn't really think, not like you probably think, not with words and language, not with a clear inner voice telling her her own thoughts there in her head; and neither do I. In that way we (me and Margaret) and those other people like us are very similar. And although we don't think as such, we do have feelings, and like you, we are conscious (when we are not unconscious, of course, say when we're asleep) and we have a sense of being, and an 'in the present' sort of 'knowing'. Knowing about the things that are familiar to us, things we can sense and experience often enough to get to properly know, in our own non-language, non-word way.

We feel, and we sense, and we know stuff, we know that we are separate from other things around us; that we are ourselves and that the other things are not. We know all that kind of stuff ... well I do, and so does Margaret, probably, although that's the difficult thing – we, me and Margaret and the people like us, we can't tell you what it is we feel and think and know, we simply can't translate it and express it in a form that we can tell to anyone else, anyone but ourselves.

You see, we have no agreed or common language that is clear enough to get that kind of complicated thinking stuff across to other people. I know I'm perhaps labouring this point a bit, but it's important. All that other people see is the way we behave, and then they have to try to work out what they think we are 'thinking', or 'feeling', as best they can. But they have no way of really knowing what's there, what's there in the inner me, no way of knowing my inner 'thoughts' (my feelings and my sensing and my knowing) because I have no way of telling them.

But I do have feelings, and I suppose, kinds of thoughts as well, not like the thoughts that you have with your inner voice thought words. No, but I do have non-word thoughts and feelings; of course I do. I have those kinds of thoughts that we probably all have, the ones that don't actually break through into clear and understandable words that you can hear your inner voice say, but even before that, you know that they are there. It's those as yet un-fully formed deeper thoughts, the ones that are under the surface, more feelings than thoughts, those are the kind of thoughts I have, and you will have as well. But unfortunately, it's impossible for me (or I suspect you) to explain the true nature of these unformed feeling thoughts, just as it must be hard for you to express your own wordless feeling thoughts to others, or even to yourself … without turning them into words to do so.

You see, as soon as you try to do that, as soon as you even try to turn these unformed thoughts into words, then they become wordy thought thoughts, and perhaps then you lose the full essence of what they originally were. They then become changed, reduced from what they were to start with into a simplified language interpretation, condensed into words that might only capture a fraction of the whole thought.

Perhaps you could try it yourself, try and switch off your chatty wordy inner voice. Look around you, feel where you are, feel what you are doing, but don't tell yourself about it: don't think about it, just do what you are doing, feel what you are feeling, just be who you are doing what you are doing, don't think anything out loud, feel it as it is as I do … no words remember … an empty head … go on, have a go … come back when you're done … go on try it, for me, for my sake, remember that it's like that all day for me, not just for a few moments … go on then … I'll wait for you here.

Actually, when you try to do it, try to think without words that is, I suspect that it probably makes it harder; it just comes naturally to me. It's who I am, and it's how I always do it, the thinking stuff. But I bet we're not that different though, because actually, I bet we all spend most of our day in that un-wordy thinking state, just going about doing what we are doing, just feeling what we are feeling, just being who we are in the world. It'll be only now and then that your wordy inner voice buts in, most of the time you'll be getting along fine without it; I guess it'd be exhausting otherwise.

So, it's only at certain times and for certain thoughts that your voice will return with wordy thoughts filling the front of your head, popping up and in with a comment or two. Apart from those certain times we're pretty much the same. I can imagine (well obviously, for arguments sake I'll have to) that there's times when you would like to switch it off, that wordy thinking voice. I bet you can easily get sick of it, that voice, chipping in with its two-penneth worth, especially if it's in a bit of mood, saying stuff you don't particularly want to hear … yes, perhaps it is sometimes less of a positive thing than you would have thought; until now!

Yes, I bet that that inner wordy voice can be a double-edged sword at times: sometimes useful, sometimes giving you pretty good ideas or some good suggestions, but at other times… well, not so good, when that less positive stuff starts, when the voice turns, and the negative stuff comes out … the drip, drip, drip of disabling self-doubt, the sharp cutting edge of repetitive self-criticism; not so good then, no, not so clever then, is it?

Well at least I'm spared that, I don't have to listen to it, although there is stuff there, feelings and flighty unfocussed un-fully formed thoughts or impressions about stuff. They are there, but they don't break through and form into your kind of words. They don't get reduced to that kind of concrete 'this means that' or 'I think precisely this' kind of thinking that words make happen in your head.

But I bet it's not that straightforward, this thinking then translating thoughts and feelings into words stuff. There's too much other stuff going on in there: feelings, senses, emotions, impressions, all there in the mix; reducing a mixture of all those vague things into a few well defined, translatable words. That can't do it all justice. Surely, we aren't that simple, surely, our thoughts, yours and mine, aren't that straightforward? Well, mine aren't, and I can't imagine that you would like to think that yours are either, not really ... surely our thinking is much messier than that, surely it is the mixed-up messiness of our different individual thoughts and minds that makes us who we are?

Surely your thinking is more than just some simple wordy thoughts chugging around inside your head, surely there is much more going on than that. Surely it is, no, surely we are more complicated and messily human than that. If it was that simple, why then would one person be so cheerful, and another so hacked off by the same sorts of things? Why would the same person be so switched on one time and so switched off the next by the same sorts of things? Where does excitement, or happiness, or boredom, or despair, where do they come from? They're not simple responses to things, somehow playing out on the surface of our minds. They come from deep down, they come from who we are, where we've come from and what we've experienced. It all gets mixed up together, and only then can it reveal even a little bit of what it truly is when we think to ourselves in words.

And what about those dark shadowy memories, almost entirely concealed. Memories of things that are long past but are still there, their churning presence lurking there in the background, prowling the unlit corridors somewhere at the back of the mind. Things that happened so long ago that you can't bring them out into the open anymore, but you know they are there, somewhere there in the foggy background, still effecting and directing your un-wordy thoughts and feelings even now, even when you can't actually locate them anywhere in your head at all. What of those? How do we account for them, and their effects on our thinking and feeling and sensing and knowing now?

What of those dislocated things and feelings that are still there, from before you can remember anything, from before you could understand anything, from before anything had become familiar? What about vague unknowable impressions about being left scared and alone, left with no one to hold you, left with no one to hold onto, left with no one to comfort you, with no one to just be with, left to just to be there, on your own in the cold caged and impenetrable dark. Where does that all go to? And why is it all still lurking around somewhere behind my feelings, here in the present?

Perhaps it's a relief that I can't think too deeply about it. I'm not sure that's the case for Margaret though?

'The songs are in your eyes
I see them when you smile
I've seen enough, I'm not giving up
On a Miracle Drug'

(U2: Miracle Drug)

The proper morning stuff is getting started ...

Yes, the morning stuff is properly getting started now... and as much as I can, in my own way, I am anticipating the usual stuff. Yes, I'm kind of looking forward, in my own quiet and relaxed way, to more or less the same day today as yesterday, and hopefully tomorrow as well, when that comes around. Yes, hopefully it will go on, over and over, with more or less the same morning sorts of things going on, and that's not a bad thing you know; not for me it isn't.

Essentially the same kind of thing, but perhaps sometimes a little bit different. Yes, more or less the same kind of thing, but perhaps sometimes in a bit of a different order, or more or less the same kind of thing with some less familiar people, or even more or less the same thing in a bit of a different place. So long as I have enough of the familiar, of the same kind of stuff going on, with enough of the essential order and pattern of my life at its heart; then it's okay. I can build an okay morning around that.

Bath time ... great ... now this is something I do like.

The soft enveloping warmth of the water, all around me, warm and wet, lovingly pushing in to even the tightest of my crevices (and believe me, I do have quite a few of them). The liberating feeling of being hoisted up, away from my own dead weight, slowly going up (after a bit of a kerfuffle of getting my night-shirt off and the netting safely under me), swinging ever so gently, twisting ever so gently, and then slowly, slowly being lowered down. The warm and tickling wetness edging up from my heels as they enter first, up the back of my legs, and then to my backside. And then it's a kind of free floaty and secure supported feeling, both at the same time. Then being gently lathered up and nicely rubbed down all over the place, and in some quite delicate places as well, the sheer joy; it makes me laugh out loud when they get it just right. Yes there, that's it, just there.

There's quite a bit of time spent on this physical rubbing bit. It feels nice, and it slowly frees me up a bit, physically that is. It helps my tight joints find a bit more give, loosens them up, so to say. The water seems a natural place for me to be, my weight and body shape less of an issue when semi-submerged … and I always feel I come out too soon. If only they could leave me in here a bit longer. So, just as I get to my maximum relaxed and limbered state, up I go, hoisted up and out, feeling the water falling away below, and the less forgiving and supportive air pushing back in amongst the crevices as the water falls away. Oh well; it was nice whilst it lasted.

The next bit's nice as well; getting rubbed dry … yes, that's pretty neat as well, being gently rubbed all over with warm and soft towels – what a great start to the day. But then, getting dressed, having my clothes put on; oh, no! No thank you! There's always a downside as well as an up, a negative queuing up to push in after a positive, restoring some kind of 'the joy of life' limiting balance; and here it comes.

Yes, getting dressed. Well, being dressed that is by someone. What a performance that is, especially those first really tight things, getting them put on to me is a real struggle, and one that I don't pretend to like. There's lots of pulling, quite a bit of stretching, both the clothes and me, and a fair amount of tugging. Lots of huffing and puffing, and that's mainly coming from the people who are doing it.

For me it is even more of a trial, and if I'm honest, I don't really try to help. It's always a bit of a battle of wills, and being me, I don't give in easily. I know it will happen whatever I do, and it always does. I'm powerless to resist, but I still can't help withholding my cooperation when it starts. I tighten up, more than normal, pull all the bits of my body in on myself, into the middle as much as I can, which admittedly isn't much.

Sometimes I take another tack, and pretend to be asleep, this being one of the few things I can do when I don't want to do something. I hold my will and my attention deep inside myself, withdraw it away from all the outside stuff, the people and all the physical stuff, the discomfort of the holding and the heaving at my limbs. But in the end the result is always the same; I'm dressed. How could it be otherwise? And maybe it's for the best. Although who's 'best' might be a point for further discussion.

It doesn't just stop when I'm dressed though. When the clothes are first put on me, after my usual futile resistance, these clothe never feel right, not to start with. They always feel too tight, and too restrictive, especially after a night in a loose and airy night-shirt, and even more so after wallowing in the physically relaxing sensations of the bath. These daytime clothes just don't sit right with me, not straight away. They press, and they squeeze, and they feel tight and knotty and uncomfortably restraining. But slowly, eventually, like every day, after a while those constricting feelings to fall away. I suppose, in a funny sort of way, it doesn't take that long for the clothes to start to disappear off of me. Their weight and pressure and knottiness seem to fade, they become less apparent and less not-quite-right, more a part of me, more a part of my movements rather than something holding me in or moving against me.

Yes, actually now that it is happening, it doesn't take long, and then the clothes somehow fade into me, rather than being on the outside, separate and distinct from me. It's like my chair really, separate and artificial when I first get put in it, but shortly afterwards it becomes an extension of me and my movements, like we have come together, blended into each other to get on with the rest of the day.

So, there it is, same every day, more or less. First of all, I am all comfortable in my night clothes, or in the bath, or having my post-bath towelling, and then at some time later, after my futile resistance, I am in my day clothes … there it is, it's a done deal, it's going to happen every day, and every day it does.

But that doesn't mean I won't continue to put up a struggle, same as every day. No, not at all. The least I can do is to make them work for it, not give in too easily, not capitulate; no one wants to be a push-over, or a pull-over; not even someone as physically feeble and limited as me. But as I say, it doesn't last long and when I stop resisting and thinking about them, then me and my clothes just seem to unconsciously make up, and just get on together … sorted out for the rest of the day. We can call it a draw then.

Oh, and then the teeth cleaning and hair combing starts …so here we go again. I won't make it easy for them. I'll make them struggle for it again, the same every day, even though I like the minty smell and taste. I'll try to keep my mouth as sealed as I can for as long as I can before they finally wheedle it in and get brushing.

Like I've probably said already, people like me need very high levels of things being done for us, and a lot of things being done to us, for almost everything we do. Not the breathing and basic physical functions, although I do need some help with that rear end pushing out kind of thing, sometimes. Although I also have times when it comes through okay … sometimes much better than okay. Actually, sometimes it comes through too well, too quickly, too much out of control, and it's really not pleasant, even though I wear special underclothing for just such eventualities.

It's when I've got something not right going on inside me. To be honest, I'd prefer not to dwell on it too much really. It's not nice; not for me, or for anyone else. But I'm utterly helpless to do anything about it, to tell people I can feel it coming, feel it brewing inside me, tell people I need help, or to ask for something to stop it.

But enough about that, it probably happens to everyone … although when it happens to me everyone knows about it, you see I can't keep it secret. And it tends to spread in a place like this. We, people like me, tend to catch stuff really rather easily, and unfortunately, we can then pass it around a bit. There's been times when it's been so bad here, we've all had it, and then everything kind of shuts down. They don't then take us out of the house, and they don't let anyone in for that matter. Although I don't suppose many people would actually be that desperate to visit us all when we're in that state, with that smell; not surprising really.

But like I say, I don't really want to dwell on that kind of business, it's a bit, well you know, a bit embarrassing (yes, maybe I occasionally do feel or get embarrassed; you can add that to my list). So, if you don't mind, that's enough said about that kind of unpleasantness, and we'll move on shall we, eh. It's nobody's fault; stuff, stuff like that, yeah, it just happens.

Now, where was I? Yes, about me needing lots of help to do almost anything and everything, all the everyday things that you'll probably take for granted, stuff that you might do for yourself, and for anyone else you have to care for. The hands on cleaning and caring stuff. The moving to and fro, the wiping and washing, the picking up, the pushing, the placing, the positioning, and the dressing and the feeding stuff, that really, truly basic everyday living kind of stuff. I need all of that doing for me. But that doesn't make me a baby or anything like that … no, I may need almost everything doing for me, totally, but I'm not a kid, not like a kid. I'm a man, a fully grown, and actually quite mature man … a man of a certain, distinguished age.

Out there in your world, sometimes people (often people who should know better) say stuff about me, and people like me.

They might say I have a 'mental age' of whatever, maybe under even one, less than a year! ... trying to compare me somehow to a baby. But really, you shouldn't take much notice of those kinds of people, to that kind of talk; it's quite misleading really. You see, it takes no account of me and my life, of my character, no account of who I actually am, of my lived experiences, and it takes no account of my acquired level of acquired personal maturity. And I'd like to think that I am really quite mature now. As mature as someone can get.

It's a very simple and lazy comparison by simple and lazy people really, as I don't think and act like a really young child. I think and act like a mature adult man who has profound and multiple learning difficulties. So why compare us, we're chalk and cheese, and I am the adult man that I have spent a lifetime becoming, it's my life's work, it's me, it's who I am. I'm not still a child; far from it.

So, if I'm not a person with a mental age of next-to-nothing, who am I then, as this mature, adult person called Harry? Well, as I've already told you, I'm a man who likes warmth, warm baths, being rubbed with a nice soft towel, cool air drifting lightly across my face, lots of different rhythmical things, the feel of my chair strap, the sound of other people's laughter nearby, citrusy smells, the feel of my muscles tightening as I raise my leg, both when it's free or against the chair leg-straps, gentle but quite high-pitched singing – especially right in, near my ear, an occasional enema, someone playing tug-o-war with me (by placing things in my hand and pulling them out again, especially if they laugh and smile and sometimes let me win). All fairly normal, everyday things. Every day for me that is, although luckily not the enemas.

I like being tickled under my chin, I like having my feet and hands massaged, I like having my own throaty mouth sounds (yes, sounds; sounds that aren't words, but are my own sounds, meaningful to me sounds) echoed back to me as if I am one equal half of a really interesting conversation, a conversation that uses my own language. I like just being with and chatting with someone using these non-word throaty sounds that I can and do make. The more folk join in with me, and echo them back to me, the more fun it is; for them and me, and the more they echo them back the more sounds I make. It's great, you ought to try it sometime.

Like I say, I like being tickled, but that, like many of the things I like, has to be done just right; not any and every kind of tickle is okay. I can also be a bit choosy about it, and I have to be in the right mood for it. But unfortunately, if and when I am in the right 'its time to get some tickles' mood, I can't actually tell people that the time is right, the time is ripe for some tickling. I can't ask them, and I can't move over to someone and lift up my chin to tell then to get on and get tickling. I only get tickled when other people decide that they would like to do it; only when they are in a tickling mood, not me.

Also, they have to be the right people, the proper tickling people, those people who are sensitive enough and are willing to work hard to try to get it right. Not too hard, not too long, not too tickly. But also, not too soft and not too short; it needs a bit of cultivating. You get the idea. It's both simple and complicated; as straightforward as you like, but as complex as, well, as I am. I'm not simple and straightforward, so neither is my preferred way of being tickled. No wonder I don't get tickled anywhere near as often as I would like, not in the ways I like best. Perhaps that's just me. Perhaps you get tickled all the time, just how you like it.

I also like it when people lie down next to me, when I'm out of my chair and on a mat, with them banging their legs in turn with me. See, I can do some things; I can bang my legs a bit. Not a lot, but a bit, and rather weakly, if I'm given the right time, enough time and the right place. Oh, and again the right person to be with; someone who knows me, who knows what to do, and who is willing to get down on the floor and do it with me. It might not seem much to you, but to me it's an enormous thing. It's one of the best ways, the most obvious ways I can show people how I feel, when I'm in a happy, silly, foot banging mood.

I also really like playing 'hide and appear' games from under towels or blankets or with people coming around from behind the back of my chair. Hiding and then suddenly appearing, as if out of nowhere. Done well, with proper timing, it's never not funny (if I'm in the right game-playing mood, that is). Admittedly the other person needs to do all the draping and holding, and quickly pulling back or moving, but it seems that it is me that brings an equal measure of joy and excitement, often accompanied by some of my best 'do it again' throaty sounds or foot-banging. No really, they couldn't do it half as well without me!

So, there are loads of things really, like I said, fairly normal things really. I like having my hands squeezed by someone, someone I like that is, and someone who likes me. I like being nudged on the elbow as if we are sharing a silly 'only known unto us' kind of joke. I like being included in a meaningless two-way conversation, that kind of thing that goes on everywhere, all the time. I'm presuming (because I have to) that that's really not much different from everyone else, but at the same time it also very, very different because of who I am. Yes, so just the same, but also very different because of how stuff has to be presented to me so that I can actually, actively be involved in some way. I don't want everything to be done for me, done to me, done around me. I want stuff done with me; in ways I can take a proper part. No, I need some stuff to do that properly involves me as an equal partner, something I can do together with someone else, with them needing me to be who I am. Yes, other people needing me; that's what I need.

That's the bit that makes it different. It's often the ordinary kind of stuff, the ordinary stuff that other people do, but it has to be done quite differently to allow me to be the same as everyone else. If I am asked to do things like everyone else, in their way, in the normal way that most people do things, usually without thinking, well, that's when I'm at my most different, that's when I stand the most apart. But when I'm doing things with other people, doing things together but in my way, as an equal partner, that's another matter. That's when I'm not really that different at all, much more the same, much more just another person, just another bloke. Yes, just another bloke, but one who happens to be in a wheelchair and who happens to have never said a single word.

Yeah, that's the interesting bit really. I need to be treated differently to be the same as everyone else, which I am really, inside. The people who are around me need to act more like me, as much like me as they can, so that I can then be just another bloke, another person just like them; then we can and do get along together just fine. And the more people act a bit (or even sometimes a lot) like me, the more I can become and act a bit more like them. Then slowly, very slowly, a bit, a tiny little bit at a time, we can come together more and more; so long as people try to act like me, make my sounds and my movements, and also like me for acting the way I do. We need to create some mutual ground to be together on and respond to each other in ways we can both understand, then we can get along just fine.

Also, I love to go out for trips in the minibus, that's one of my most favourite things, trips out in the minibus, strapped in the back, my chair bolted to the floor, and then off we go. All the combined sensations of familiar smells, sights, sounds and then the lovely free flowing motion seem to come together in just the right way. The dusty musty smell, the enveloping mixture of light and shadow, the rhythmical rocking and knocking noises, the steady stream of pictures constantly moving across the windows, the deep-felt, sensuous sensations of effortless motion, up and down, side to side, forward and then again, further forward.

I can just sit back, be still and go with the physical flow, and enjoy it. Relaxation and stimulation, such a potent, thrilling, soothing mix blended all together ... and the feelings of enclosure and security; the absence of unwanted demands for me to do anything or have anything done to me. Yes, I really do like trips in that minibus, they suit me just fine. I'll be asleep in no time.

But for now, all clean, dry and dressed, as every day, I've been pushed into the warm busy food room, and with a rustle of my hair, parked up looking across and out of the big clear window. The outside is bright, and the inside is sweet smelling and noisy in an inviting and comforting way. Nice rhymical noises come from something in the corner. Not words, just sounds that move together nicely; that dance together as if they've repeatedly and painstakingly practiced all the moves. Sounds that don't want a response, sounds that make no demands but give out a friendly welcome, without saying why or how. I'll be okay here for a while.

The smell of the morning ...

Hmm, yes, this is the smell of the morning. Creeping across quietly, the waft of the morning's aroma floating gently in, under my nose ... the smell I remember, the smell of the house fully waking up, the smell of the day really getting going: cooked bread and porridge. But that won't be for me; that will be for someone else, not me, not now. You see, I don't get to eat any of this sweet-smelling food. No, they don't feed me. No, not anymore, not like they used to, not through my mouth that is. That's because my food now goes straight into my belly. Yes, I know, straight there; fed through a tube that takes the stuff straight into my stomach.

It's a strange feeling, being hungry, or feeling thirsty, then not eating anything, but instead having stuff pushed in, straight into your stomach. Then almost immediately, there I am not feeling hungry or not feeling thirsty, not anymore, and not really knowing what it was that changed the situation.

Imagine that, almost like magic, a rub on the head, a few sounds said, a tap on the belly and wham, feeling full, but with no tasting, no chewing, no swallowing. But all of a sudden, full and sort of satisfied, without really feeling satisfied, which I did when I was allowed to eat my food the old-fashioned way, with my mouth.

So now the smell of food and mealtimes aren't quite what they were. Actually, nowhere near, especially when you only have very limited ways of taking real pleasure from the world, only a few things in life that really do it for you, things you can really look forward to. To lose breakfast, dinner, tea, and supper, those familiar pleasure points that make up and punctuate a day … and all the snacks and other bits of stuff, biscuits, ice creams, sweets, crisps, and all the drinks: tea, coffee, that really fizzy stuff that tickles your nose, that beer stuff, all fruity and frothy, all of it gone. Gone, just like that, never to return. Well, to put it very mildly, that's a lot to lose, and it takes a bit of getting used to. Yes, a bit of getting used to indeed.

It's making my mouth water just thinking about it, thinking about food, just having that toast and porridge smell circling around me and edging in up my nose. And I do think about it, food that is, I have the memory of it, and that memory is continually rekindled by the smells. I can smell it now, and I still kind of know, have vaguely impressiony type memories of what it used to be like. To eat food, to have it in my mouth, to chew and taste it, to feel satisfied by it.

So, I know it's around me while its being cooked, for everyone else, it makes my mouth wet. Then though, I'll have to wait, with the smell and the time weighing in on me. Then they'll finally get around to pushing my stuff straight into me, down my tube, through my stomach hole and into my belly; and its done. Yes, in through a tube, straight in, filling me up, satisfying my hunger and my thirst, but not getting rid of my memory of the pleasure, of the anticipation, of my wish to taste, and chew and savour. It's just not the same. It's a lot of life to miss out on!

To be honest though (and remember, I always am) perhaps my memory of eating is made up of all the best bits. In reality, eating wasn't always that pleasant. When I say eating, I mean being fed, and then eating. No, the being fed bit, obviously by someone else, wasn't always something to savour. Sometimes, actually often, it all came in a bit too fast, not giving me a proper chance to fully chew it, taste it and savour it. Sometimes being fed, before my stomach tube was fitted, I wasn't always given chance to properly catch my breath, to do any savouring. Sometimes it was one spoonful coming in right after the other, and then again, the next one following on just a bit too quick, just a bit too fast for me to really keep up with. I didn't have enough time to chew it properly, even though it was always mashed up into a soft pulp already, so that I could swallow it easier. It doesn't sound great does it. It wasn't the best way to savour the taste, to let my food playfully tease my palate. No, no, not at all, in it went, one urgent spoonful after another.

It's no wonder some of it ended up going back the way it came, falling down my chin, or sometimes right out and down my front … or worse. Sometimes some of it would get stuck, small bits would; they'd sometimes get stuck at the back corners of my jaw, round the sides of my teeth, under my lips. Then it would be hard to get it back into the proper swallowing part of my mouth. Or worse still, sometimes bits of food would get caught up in the top part of my throat, irritating the bits at the back, making me hack it back so that it would be coughed up and out all over the place … not nice. No, not nice; not nice for me, and not nice for anyone sat near me either.

Then sometimes the tiny bits of food I coughed up would be drawn back in on my next gasping breath and end up getting swiftly sucked down into my lungs. Down deep, really deep, past the coughing bits we have at the top. Foody little droplets getting drawn in and down as I coughed and wheezed and coughed again. Just a few tiny bits, creeping in undetected with those rasping gasps. They were the silent ones, getting in amongst the coughing, and staying once the coughing stopped. Getting right down in there, down into the bottom of my chest; tiny bits of food, little drops of drink, and there they would stay for a while, annoying me, tickling away before turning on me.

When it went bad, it started off as that, just a small tickly feeling; not too bad, something I'd been quite used to. But sometimes, as time went on it got to feel bigger and bigger, the presence and feel of it; just sitting there, just biding its time. It's not a nice feeling, you want to kind of cough, but there's nothing there to cough out. It's like having an itch and not being able to scratch it (and I'm quite used to that as well). Then, slowly and gently, it starts to burn. A sickly heat would build inside my chest, getting warmer, getting sicklier. And there it would stay, no matter what I'd do, which wasn't much, but it was as much as I could. And sometimes the burning would spread out from my chest and take over my whole body, even my head. Those weren't nice times, the sickly tickling warmth inside my chest times. Then I didn't want to eat, with it sitting there right inside, burning away, sapping all my energy, all my appetite. But I couldn't tell anyone. I suppose they had to guess.

Actually, one time it got so bad, so regular, the 'too quick' spooning and shovelling in, and then the coughing and the wheezing, that I just stopped eating. I was getting anxious before it even started, in anticipation, before the first spoon arrived. So, I just stopped opening my mouth for them, I stopped them shovelling it in. In the end I nearly starved myself. Yes, properly starving I was, not eating at all, and hardly drinking. As soon as I knew what was coming, when I was about to be fed, I'd clamp my mouth tight shut, and so for ages I hardly ate anything at all. It became a battle of wills, because that was all I had to use against them; all I had to tell them to stop. It was them wanting me to eat, wanting to feed me, and me holding my lips tight shut to stop them.

I'm not sure why I started doing it really, it wasn't a thought through tactic or anything, it just kind of happened. But it started with the anxious feeling. That was getting worse, and it had started to come on even before the first spoon was forced into my mouth. When someone sat next to me, when I smelled the food under my nose, then I sensed that something unpleasant was going to happen, and then my appetite went. At that moment I didn't feel hungry anymore, and so I didn't open my mouth. I just didn't fancy it, and I didn't want it in my mouth, I wasn't hungry, because I was too anxious about what was going to happen, the feeling of what was coming, of losing control. So, I suppose I took control in the only way I could - I didn't open my mouth. And afterwards I didn't feel any worse. Not at the end of it: no coughing, no wheezing, no burning in the chest.

I didn't always win though. Some staff would hold my nose, holding it so that I couldn't breathe, trying to get me to open up for them, to open my mouth so that they could shovel it in. I would try, really try to hold it back, my breath, but I couldn't. I couldn't hold out, and as soon as I opened my mouth to gasp in a gulp of air, in came the spoon. Wham, quick as a flash, open, in, cough, shut again; until the next spoonful was ready, and the fingers came back to clamp my nose shut. But it only seemed to make me more determined, more resistant, and anyway, it also made me cough all the more when they did get some food in.

The more they tried to force food into my mouth, the more anxious I became, so that I even started to get anxious when I smelled any food around me, even other people's. Anxious that it might be for me, might be forced on me. So, it all went around in a circle, with all that anxiety making me even less hungry, less inclined to eat, and therefore even more determined to do something to stop it, to try to take some kind of control. So, on top of closing my mouth, I then started moving my head from side to side, as best I could, trying to dodge them, to make myself a moving target, trying to do my best to make it difficult to get hold of me, to force the food in me.

I suppose they might have been doing it for the best reasons, trying their best for me in some strange way. But I didn't know that (how could I?), and it didn't feel like that to me. And therefore, it just spiralled downwards. Eventually they stopped though, they stopped the nose holding, and the shovelling in. By that time, I was beginning to head downhill, feeling tired in my body and in my head. It was getting worse; with me not eating, not feeling well, and not having any wish to eat.

But yes, then they stopped. I'm not sure why, but they let me win. Yes, I think I won that one. I came out on top, and then slowly, after a while, my appetite returned, a bit. But they stopped trying to feed me, they never did it again, ever. Instead, I acquired this tube thing in my belly. One day, while I was asleep, I ended up with a hole down there, and in it all goes, easy as you like. And since then, if I'm honest, the coughing and wheezing and burning thing has been much better.

But I do sometimes sort of remember the nice times of eating, with the nice smells around me. The anxiety has now gone as nothing bad happens to me anymore. None of the nose holding or shovelling in; the nice food memories seem to have returned and taken over. You see, some people, the ones who knew me well, they knew my pace, and they went at my pace, at an okay speed for me to keep up and enjoy it, really savour and enjoy my food. But too often it was people who didn't really know me, people who weren't sure what to do or how to do it, people trying to get it over with as soon as possible. All that coughing and wheezing. Talk about dying for something to eat, well quite a few times I nearly did. No, those times weren't nice. I don't miss that. But I do now sort of miss those nice food times, now that they have returned and forced the others to the back of my food associated memory.

They still wet my lips, and that's nice, but there are no more battles, no more teeth clenching and head shaking, no more nose holding and shovelling, no more nearly choking, no more itching and burning in my chest. Although I do have my appetite back, it goes once they put the food into the tube, it's gone in no time. Not ideal I suppose, but at least it's better than the shovelling, coughing and chest-burning alternative.

So, where were we? Ah, yes, I was telling you about the smell, and how it makes me want to eat, well to feel full anyway, full of food. And just at the right time, the same time every day, here it comes. My name is said, my shirt is lifted, there's a little bit of pushing and pulling, and then in it goes … and I'm full. Quick, clean and very efficient, but not very tasty, nothing to feel in the mouth, nothing to savour; and I'm suddenly full.

Ahh, here she comes …

Ahh, here she comes, coming to sit next to me, pulling a chair up, fetching across the big sheets of stuff that she likes to unfold and stare at. And she seems to like to share it with me. I don't know why she likes to look at this stuff and talk to me at the same time, but there seems to be something really important about it; something that she feels she has to tell me.

It's quite nice really, I feel somehow included in this, her activity, sharing short bursts of stuff that seems meaningless to me, but important to her. I'm kind of on the outside of this activity, but I like it just the same. It's now become part of my familiar routine. She does this every time she's here, and there is something about the tone of her sounds that gently hints at positive possibilities, some lovely surprises, a nice something for somebody sometime soon.

So, she is settling down now, right by my side, the thin sheety thing is unfolded, and she is shuffling and shifting herself into position. Then she starts:

"Okay Harry, let's have a look at what's going to happen for you … it's Sagittarius isn't it, okay, let's see …

"Well, it says here that 'Mars is in the ascendant, therefore soon you will be shown how much you can achieve if you're open to all possibilities' … but it also says 'don't be too hasty and remember to stay focused on issues in your personal life or you could miss out on something wonderful'.

"Well, that sounds interesting, perhaps you're going to do something really great today, do something to really show yourself, to really show us all, eh Harry.

"It goes on Harry, it says, 'learn to trust your instincts when it comes to romance', and 'someone you meet soon may just be that special someone to take notice of'.

"Oh Harry, did you hear that, 'that special someone to take notice of' ... I knew it Harry, you lucky fella, I wonder who that's going to be ... who's the lucky lady going to be I wonder?

"But there's more, it says to 'look out for trouble at work as there are some important changes ahead, so be sure to be the one to take a lead when the changes happen'. Changes eh Harry, well there's always changes, that's for sure, definitely right about that ... and according to this we'll all be looking to you to sort it out ... ahhh!"

So, what am I supposed to make of all that then? Is it supposed to be relevant? Is it supposed to be somehow meaningful? It's certainly directed at me, but is it supposed to show me some sort of deeper truth about her, or me, or the world around us? To me it just sounds like a right load of "blah, blah, blah and yet more blah".

But who am I to say anything about it; after all I can't actually say anything at all. These sounds might be the most insightful and important words ever uttered, by anyone. But like I say, or better, I sense, it all sounds empty, devoid of any significant meaning, well to me it does anyway. But none-the-less, taken

82

together as a whole, as a thing to just listen to, it all sounds quite nice, even if I don't get anything of the drift.

Still, it is nice because I sense that it is directed at me, with the warm and friendly sounds coming in my direction. There is something really positive, really engaging and interesting about how she tells me this stuff. Yeah, I like that kind of talk, I like to feel a part of it. I like to be involved. Her tone of voice says she wants me to listen, to be a part of this activity. It's as if this lady really, genuinely wants me to be part of her conversation. So yes, I think that's okay, despite all the meaningless words, it's the tone and the focus on me that makes it okay. It feels like it's better for her that I hear what she has to say, so that's also nice as well. Having that part to play; being a bit important, even if I don't have a single idea of how.

Actually, if I'm honest, from where I sit and what I see, a lot of the stuff that goes on for other people, the things they seem to do, well most of it seems entirely pointless. Perhaps it is actually pointless, perhaps it's meant to be, perhaps that is the point of it … after eating, drinking, breathing and clearing yourself out, all the other stuff that other people do doesn't seem to have much real reason for it, not that I can see. Nothing much seems to come from most of the things they seem to keep themselves busy doing.

So perhaps they just do it to fill up all the time they have between the life keeping going stuff. Perhaps they just do it when they aren't doing the proper and important living stuff to keep the mind-bending weight of empty time at bay. Perhaps saying this stuff out loud, like this lady does every day, is one of those in-between, empty time avoiding things. Perhaps doing lots and lots of pointless things is somehow preferable to being, well whatever the alternative is. Perhaps people fill up their time by doing these pointless things because it's simply better than not doing them.

And really, from where I sit, there doesn't seem to be much more point to a lot of the things I see other people doing. These other people spend a lot of time sitting in front of the flickering sound and light coming out from the telly box thing, or they sit looking at pictures of other people in those papers. They often stand opposite each other and speak with words I don't understand, but then just stop without doing anything and then move away from each other. They do this talking at each other loads and loads and loads of times, every day. Surely there can't be that much that needs saying over and over again to the same people, every day, day in day out.

It all looks pretty repetitive, pretty monotonous, pretty pointless and unproductive to me ... although there is a difference, because no one tries to stop them doing their things, no one thinks that their things are pointless and a waste of time and therefore a negative thing that needs to be stopped, like some of the stuff that I do.

So yes, I do a lot of stuff that fills up the time I have when I'm not doing the proper and important required for living stuff. I'm not doing that now, because I have a bit of company, and I'm listening to and watching (as best I can) the stuff that's going on around me. But at other times I do do pointless stuff to fill my time. Perhaps we're not so different again here, eh?

Sometimes I play with the strap on my chair; sometimes I slowly move my head from one side to the other; sometimes I grind my teeth really loudly; sometimes I push myself back into my chair; sometimes I force my best leg up against the strap of my chair when it is pulled up tight across my shin.

That's funny that, well perhaps only in a funny kind of way. It's funny that when I'm relentlessly exploring my chair strap, or repeatedly pushing my good leg out against the tight leg strap, or persistently moving my head slowly back and forth I feel different to when I'm still, inactive and just a disconnected observer of the stuff going on around me. There is something about being engaged in those familiar, simple and repetitive activities that absorbs an important part of my consciousness, that removes me from my other inner, deeper thoughts and feelings. And actually, when you think about these pointless things, perhaps that's exactly the point?

These things I do, the things that look very different from what many other people do, the repetitive moving, the repeated pushing against, the grinding, all those sorts of things, well, they somehow free me from the rest of my existence, they add some recognisable and calming stimulus to my central being and distract me from the continuous flow of moments that I sometimes feel might overwhelm me. Sorry, I feel that I'm getting all kind of profound here, but I think that if I faced them unprotected by some kind of absorbing activity, they could become intolerable.

And for me, in my chair, there is always an abundant supply of these long empty moments of time, the ones that seem to carry the sheer mass of all creation with them. There's loads of them actually, streaming through, moment after moment, unremitting in their arrival, and perhaps it's not so different for these people, for this lady with the paper.

Yes, perhaps these other people feel the same at times, the same as me … otherwise why do they do all their pointless stuff?

'Of science and the human heart
There is no limit
There is no failure here sweetheart
Just when you quit'

(U2: Miracle Drug)

I can sometimes see my own reflection …

I can sometimes see my own reflection in the living room window. That's where I'm usually put after the first eating, or not eating, part of the day has been finished with. The room has a whole wall made only of glass, and when the lights are on inside, and it's a bit dark outside, and if my chair is positioned in the right direction, and before they pull the curtains, then I think I can see an image of myself, reflected back to me by this window wall. I can then spend quite some time trying to look directly at myself, trying hard to see this strange mainly chair-shaped figure, which is somehow in some way me (and actually yes, I think I really do know that it is somehow a connected representation of me, but not really me). So, I can sometimes spend quite a bit of time trying really hard to see how I am, and how I move (which isn't much to be honest) in the time that I am both here and there.

When I watch myself, I slowly move my head around, and so does this ghostly figure in the window, this other me … I like it, it feels a bit weird, a bit 'out-of-body', but it's great. I try to do that thing I do with my leg, move it up and shake it. I do that when I am feeling a bit giddy, a bit excited. I say I do it, but really it kind of does it itself, my leg that is. Actually, it's just my right leg, it somehow knows when I am feeling giddy, and it then it gets giddy all of itself. That's when it starts to shake and kick out, somehow expressing my inner giddiness with a burst of excited movement. It just does it, but also it kind of feels right, I mean, to me it feels right, like it is expressing something on my behalf. Go for it leg, that's what I say … well obviously I don't say that, I don't say anything, but my leg is saying the stuff for me, and that's okay by me, it saves doing the job myself.

Anyway, sometimes with this reflection thing, I will look at it for a while, and quite nonchalantly I will slowly look away, and then, when I think it isn't ready, that other me, I will quickly look back to see if I can catch it out, to see if I can beat it and see the back of my head ... but I haven't managed it yet.

I say all this stuff about looking, and seeing, and all that, but actually I often have to struggle really hard to control my eyes, to make them look where I want them to. They often do a bit as they wish, and they can roll right back, up into my head, and this happens most if I don't have anything interesting to look at, like when I'm in front of the light and sound telly box. Then my eyes can take on a life of their own, a bit like my leg really, rolling up and down and around with a will of their own. When that happens, when it's really bad, I can only catch fleeting glimpses of the things I'm trying to look at, even if they are straight in front of me. But if something or somebody catches my eye (so to speak), and its not too far away, then, with a real effort, I can calm the demons within them and focus my eyes in on whatever or whoever it is ... if it's still enough and interesting enough, and if it stays where it is for long enough.

Actually, that's quite a reliable way for people to know if something is interesting enough for me to be interested in, for an observant bystander to get a sense that whatever or whoever it is doing something, whether it is sufficiently interesting to draw and hold my visual attention. If it can stop my eyes from dancing around or wandering off, then yes, it is interesting enough for me. If my eyes are darting about all over the place, disappearing up and away under their lids, then no, it isn't right, it isn't sufficiently interesting … perhaps you should think about changing it (whatever, or whoever it is!).

Sometimes though, I can be a bit naughty with this eye thing. Sometimes, just sometimes, if I can't be bothered with people and for some reason, and I want them to leave me alone, I just shut my eyes and pretend to be asleep. It's a bit of cheat really, a bit unfair, but it's the best way I have of controlling other people's access to me, the inside me, the actual me that knows what's going on and whether I want to be a part of it, or not. So that's what I sometimes do, just shut my eyes and pretend not to be in. Hopefully, and usually, people don't hang around long then, and I will then open them up when I think they've gone.

I can also play this eye shutting business like a game, with half an eye occasionally opened to catch anyone who might be around and looking. It's a bit like that suddenly appearing game, coming visible out of nowhere, but designed especially for me. I can play it from my end without actually moving, well only moving one eyelid very slightly … but for me that's pretty impressive, the physical and mental control required is quite something.

To be honest though, much of the stuff I do remains a mystery to me, as to why I do it; I just tend to do it, whatever it is. Again, being honest (when am I ever anything other?) my deep-seated motives, the reasons why I do some stuff, why I sometimes behave as I do, well, I really can't explain it, not even to myself. But to be honest, again, that should come as really no surprise; to either of us.

Perhaps other people, people like you are different. Perhaps you, and other people like you really do know why they do the stuff they do, but I don't, not fully. I kind of am aware of some of it, I kind of have a sense that this feels nice, or I don't fancy that, but that doesn't account for most of the things I do. Perhaps other people, people like you, are different. Perhaps other people are always clear about why they do the things they do and are therefore always self-aware and able to control it all, be able to do the things they want, at the times they want, and in the circumstances they want. And not do things they don't want.

Perhaps other people can do all that, fully control themselves and their behaviours. But I can't, sometimes, well always really, I just find myself doing it, the behaviour or whatever it is, before I have had time to know what it is that I should or could do in the circumstances. So, by the time I kind of know what I should or could be doing, by then I'm already doing it, whatever it is, the behaviour has already started, and it's too late then to stop it. Perhaps other people are different, perhaps they are more aware of their own behaviour and can control themselves better than me? Yes, perhaps?

Actually, sitting here near the window, I am starting to feel quite warm now, inside that is, warm and a bit sticky, under my chin. The light from outside is getting really quite bright, and its making me feel a bit too warm. The light is getting into my eyes, a lot of it, too much really. I don't think my eyes like this much light, not all in one go, and so I'm going to have to shut them again and keep them shut to keep the light out from where it isn't welcome.

But there isn't much I can do but sit here, in my chair, and hope that I get moved to a cooler, shadier spot. And actually, ohh, here we go … I'm moving now. That was quick, someone must have spotted me, thought I look a bit miffed, or something, and so I'm getting moved somewhere else, and I hope it's somewhere where the light isn't as bad. And the too much warmth isn't too bad as well.

Yes, so I'm now over here, and the light and the heat and the stickiness are better here … I haven't moved far, but the light and the heat haven't followed me across, they must have stayed over there, and now I'm over here, where the light and the warmth and the stickiness are now okay. That's better. Parked up again, but in a more comfortable place; the climate here is much more to my liking.

Sometimes, actually quite often, I will remain in the same place for quite a long time. Yes, sometimes I have to remain there, wherever there is, for what seems like ages, and I can't do anything about it. Left to be in one place, being there in the same place surrounded by the same things … and sometimes I quite like that. It depends on how long, so not too long that the time starts to weigh, and it depends on my mood. If I'm in the right laid-back kind of mood, then being in the same place for a while can be quite nice. So, like many things, it just depends.

If I feel okay, not too hot, not too cold, not too bothered by any other people around me, sometimes being in the same place for long enough gives me the opportunity to sense things around me, to take a long look, or a long feel of it, a long experience of whatever it is that's going on. I can sense the patterns in the light, or focus in on the noises that are there, I can smell the air that sits in the place, and so I can sense the overall feel of the place and how comfortable and safe I feel in it. It usually takes me quite a while to pull all this together, to be able to fully focus on all these things, with all my senses working together, and I need to be properly awake to do it (I do tend to doze off too easily at times).

Some places certainly do have a good sense or feel to them if the smell and the light and noises are all okay, all in balance with each other, not too much, and not too little, and then I feel happy to be there, wherever it is. If the balance is right, the light and smell and noise just right, that's when a place feels okay and comfortable for me to be in. I can enjoy those times, in one place, with not too much going on, but just enough. Then it gives me a chance to get my bearings, a chance to get familiar with what is around me, to get a sense of the light and the smell and the noise, to know that that I have been here before, that it is still part of my familiar house, part of my familiar world, connected by a doorway to the place I was before I came here … because it is, and it's one of the things I know best.

Being me in my familiar house; well, with all the practice I've had, that is my area of real expertise.

Now it's time for a bit of a rest …

Yes, it's now time for a bit of a rest, a bit of down time … for all of us here, the folk that live here, and have been woken, bathed, dressed and fed, and for the people who care for us. They are all sat in the kitchen now, around the table, nattering away, saying those things over and over to each other, having their own drinks, and I'm in the front room, parked in front of the sounds and light telly box. I'm comfy now, away from the window wall, at least for a while. This telly box thing though, I don't think it's always been around. If I could properly remember my younger days, I don't think I would remember such a thing. So perhaps there was a time before it came along, before it became our almost constant, go to companion. I can't actually remember that time, it seems to have been with us for so long, it's like part of the family, our family here, but I reckon it's not always been there. Well not as big and bright and as always 'on' as it is now.

I'm not complaining, because I'm not that kind of man, well mostly not. At first the telly thing was a small flickering box that only came on later in the day, before bedtime, and then only for a short time, with colourless flashing pictures. But then they started getting bigger, and bigger, and bigger, and they started being on for longer, and longer, and the then all colours came, and then kept getting brighter, and the pictures started flashing past faster and faster, with the sounds seeming to come from different directions, not just from the actual telly box itself.

Anyway, I don't really watch it, not as such. None of us do. We might be physically sat in front of it, we might be looking in the general direction of it, but I don't pay it any attention really. To me, if you've seen one bit of this telly stuff, you've seen it all. It all seems to be just the same as what was on yesterday, and the day before, and the day before that; perhaps it is.

But I don't get much from it, not really … perhaps it isn't here for us, perhaps it's on more for the other people, the people who come here to help us, to look after us, perhaps they brought it here. Perhaps that's why we have it, perhaps it's part of their family and they would miss it too much if they couldn't have it here with them. Or perhaps it needs caring for like we do? Who knows? certainly I don't; but they seem to give it quite a bit of attention at times, so perhaps that's it.

Actually, I haven't said much, or anything really, about the people who look after us here, the people who are around us and with us for most of the day. So, what do I think about them, these other people who are always around me, washing me, feeding me, dressing me, pushing me around? you might well ask; perhaps you already have.

Well, I find them a bit of a mixed bunch really, all a bit different, they all have their own particular smells, and their own particular ways of doing stuff, different ways of getting close, different ways of giving touch, different ways of being themselves. Some are big and some quite small, some are thin and some quite wide, some are dark and some quite light, some are hairy, and some aren't, some talk with deep voices, and some don't, some are soft and friendly and take time over things, and well, to be honest, some don't.

I don't really blame them. It can't be easy, what with all the lifting up, and the pushing and pulling, the feeding and the dressing, the bathing and the other stuff, the cleaning up and wiping down. So, I shouldn't be too critical. I'm not sure I could or would want to do this kind of thing myself, to other people, if I were able to, if things were the other way around. Maybe I would, and maybe I'd enjoy it, maybe I'd be good at it, but maybe I wouldn't. I don't know. How could I?

But about the staff, yes, they are a mixed bunch, different in lots of ways, and I do have favourites amongst them, the people I prefer to be with, and it is often those that seem to like being with me. I probably shouldn't have favourites, they are all trying to help me to some extent, but I do, that's just how it is. Actually, it is hard to work out why some people seem to suit me better than others, and it can't always be because of an overly generous chest area (and I'm not complaining if they have what you might describe as a fuller, more generous figure; in my experience, which is all I have to go on, it often seems to go along with a warm and caring and somehow physically more enveloping person behind it).

But there are some staff, staff who too often tend to work on me, rather than with me, they tend to talk at me or over my head, too often mainly talking to each other and only sometimes focussing fully on me, the person they are doing something to. Yes, and those same people only seem to spend time with me when they need to do something to me or for me. They don't seem to be there at other times, when it might be nice to just have someone around for company rather than of necessity.

I'm hoping that you're coming to know me a bit now, to know that I'm generally not one to grumble, but sometimes it is a little irritating. The main thing is that I can't do anything about it. I do think that it's something to do with my general position as a person in relation to other people, in the social ordering of things. It's like when people just switch away from me to talk to someone else who has just come in the room, or if they dash off in the middle of doing something, like feeding me, to talk into that phone contraption, or when they take out their ever-present hand phone things to look at its small screen or frantically tap the front of it for five minutes before resuming what they were (and should still be) doing with me.

Maybe as I'm getting older, I'm starting to moan a bit more, and yes of course, technically I am middle-aged, so maybe moaning just starts to creep out a bit more easily, a bit more often. But, well sometimes, and it is just sometimes, and it is just with some people, well, they could put more into it, invest a bit more of themselves into doing what they're doing, and do it properly for me and with me, not just to me. That's all I ask; that's my main grumble, just sometimes.

But on the whole, to be honest, the staff who look after me, with just the occasional exception, are really good, really very good, really very good to me. For the most part I couldn't actually want for better staff. But there are a few, those one's who I sense their hearts aren't really in it, not in properly caring, doing caring stuff in a properly caring way. But thankfully they're the exception.

Actually, some of the good ones are even better than good. They're the staff who have a bit of something more about them, they are the ones who mean much more to me. As well as doing all the physical caring stuff, they are real friends to me, warm and giving rather than just being just a bit cool and detached in what they do, in how they care for me. I love to be with those people, I love them, I do, and I love to have them around me. I hope that's the same for them, and I really keenly sense that it is. That feeling I get, it feels true to me. I hope they get that feeling back from me, in the best ways I can give it out. I really do hope that they sense it too.

It's interesting though, how different they all are, how differently they care for me, and how different they can be with me. Some of the staff seem to put on a high-pitched, singsongy voice when they talk to me. I'm not sure why, but they do, and some start speaking much louder, and some much more slowly. Some talk to me with a constant laugh in their voice, and some people talk to me by going much higher at the high bits with their voice and much lower at the lower bits. It is interesting, really interesting, how they seem to change their sounds for me, much more interesting for me as the person who is listening.

That kind of talking seems to mean so much more, the sounds that is, not the words. I can't really work out what they mean, but there is something about the slow, clear, up and down sounds, happy sounds, as if just for me, clear sounds, catching my attention, the speaker giving me their full attention, giving me a full range of sounds to listen to with their voice. Yes, that is interesting, for me, with the words not meaning anything much, but the clear, slow, singsongy, happy sounds making some kind of sense to me, because they are just right, just for me. I like those people best of all, those people who change things just for me, with their clear, slow, happy sounds done just for me. Those people working with me, caring for me, at my level. Yes, that is interesting for me, and I can sense how they feel towards me when they do that.

It's all about building that feeling, that relationship between us, that's what's important. Some can do it and some can't, well, not as well. It's more than just making the different kinds of sounds. There's other stuff as well, and I can't always clearly sense what it is. But some people just have different somethings about them; some people play different roles, some just care, but some people are playful and cheeky and matey, and some are warm and close and enveloping – some of them with big soft chests. Have I mentioned I like those big soft chests before? Well, I do like them, I like big soft and enveloping chests that push into me when some people lean over me to do stuff for me. Sometimes they come right in and even push in right across my face! Wow, what a lovely thing! Although perhaps it's wrong of me to mention this? What with having some people as my favourites to be around because of the big and soft chest things. Sorry if I offend those without, with a smaller and less enveloping chest, but honesty and all that, the best policy and all that … yes, I do like that when it happens.

Although it isn't always lovely warm and caring chests and everything. Sometimes, some of my people can be a bit stern and serious with me at times, although sometimes, if I'm honest, that's probably the right thing for me when I'm being contrary. But some other people, sometimes they can be nicely quiet and calm, with just an odd word in my direction. Sometimes they're nicely loud and excited, creating a loud and exciting atmosphere for me to be part of and enjoy. Sometimes some of them are more physically engaging, tapping and stroking me, ruffling my thinning hair. Others are sometimes up and more active, moving me around, twisting me around in my chair, getting me going; there's all sorts really.

I can't always say, actually, obviously, I can never say what it is that makes me and some people just hit it off. It's a bit like the chap that sometimes, at bedtime, well he quietly kneels down next to me, bows his head and says some words into his hands that seem to be about me, or for me, or something. And he does it in a really nice and easy way, with lovely rhythmical and repeating words that seem to encircle me and somehow, because of the tone of his voice, they make me feel safe and special. Don't ask me how; how would I know, but they just do.

It seems to be the way that he does it, not what he is doing that makes the difference. That's what seems to count, the way that something's done. But how do you describe that, that special way, that certain quality of doing or being a bit more there. It being a bit deeper, somehow more concentrated, it being a bit more rooted in the moment, capturing that quality of the time, using its weight to good effect so that it doesn't hang heavy on you, but somehow brings an intensity that fixes you there in that moment. Or is it something about the familiarity of what he's doing, or just of him? It's complicated I know … and it doesn't seem to change anything, but its nice whilst it lasts, and it relaxes me into the night.

It really does take all sorts to make a world, to make my world that is, that's for sure … and it really does take all sorts to make a group of caring people, and a group of carers and friends. They're all a bit different in what they do, in who and how they are and how they care for me, and amongst them there are those special people who I love. I hope they love me back; I really do think they do.

Anyway, enough about them. This is my book, so let's get back to talking and thinking about me. Yes, I'm still here in front of the telly box. To be honest, it isn't really doing anything for me, so perhaps now's a good time for a little nap. Afterall, I didn't sleep well last night; I rarely do, not all night. I'm often awake then, so I often fall asleep during the day. So yes, that's the thing, it feels like that's the best thing. Afterall, I've had a busy morning, and there's nothing really going on for me now, in this moment.

I can already feel some of the tiredness pushing through from where it hides behind my eyes, they're getting a little bit heavier. I can feel the effort of all this morning's activity catching up with me, what with the getting up, the being bathed, the being dressed, the being fed. If I just let myself go with it, and if I just shut my eyes for a couple of minutes ... I'll just have a short nap, just shut my eyes for a moment or two.

It's not like I'm missing anything. It's only the telly, it's not like I'm ... it's not ... it's ...

Oh, still here are you ...

Oh, still here are you? ... sticking with it, eh. Well thanks for that, I appreciate that, and it was only a short nap, wasn't it. In fact, I think we seem to be growing quite close now, having shared so much stuff between us ... we are, aren't we? Well, from my perspective I feel I'm getting to trust you, what with you sharing my space, my world, being here with me, sharing a bit of my life. I'm getting to feel quite comfortable with it all, I hope you are.

So, now that we trust each other, perhaps now's the time to be a bit more open, perhaps we could give air to a few difficult truths and possibly confront ourselves with some challenging issues. My life now is different to what it was, and different again to how things used to be. So perhaps now would be a good time, if any time is good for such things.

Yes, perhaps it might be useful to look a bit more deeply into the time that went before, at some of the stuff that has gone on for people like me, at the hands of people like you. Yes, perhaps it would be good, or at least useful to think about other people like me, people with really severe stuff wrong with them, most of them no longer with us.

Let's just have a think about all those people, people like me, who have mainly been locked well away from the rest of you. Put away somewhere, put away from everyone else in hospitals or asylums or colonies, whatever you call them, or whatever they were or still are called by the less caring amongst you. Not you, oh goodness me, no. I'm certainly not pointing a finger at you; you're still reading this book, so that should say something about you. That certainly counts in your favour.

But there have been others, and plenty of them, who thought it best to keep us all apart; and to be honest, many still do. To keep us, well, people like me, and people like you well away from each other. Really well away, so well away that we could never actually meet, not unless you deliberately came out of your world and into mine … and that didn't happen much, no, not really, not very much at all.

Also, some people, some who thought that we were so different, so different from everybody else that we should be kept apart, well, they had some really strong ideas about how they should treat us, people like me that is, and where and how we should live and behave. Yes, they often had plenty of ideas about us, and about how to treat us.

It probably starts off with ways they think they can help us be more like them. This is all stuff I don't understand, but some of it has been done to me. Luckily, I can't remember most of it; well all of it really. Not in any detail. But sometimes other people would repeated ask a more powerful unseeable force (or person or being) to make us 'better', that being to make us more like them. They would say or sing stuff over us or sometimes take us along to a special place with the promise of some more singing and a cup of tea and biscuits. Sometimes we were taken in a very big minibus a very long way to a very special place where they would splash us with some special water so that we might be made into someone else, someone more normal.

And there were others who might sit next to people like me, and push and pull at our elbows so that we (not them) would knock on a board with funny lines on it, and then apparently we (not them) would go on to write a whole letter ... or even a lovely poem, and then we (not them) would apparently be able to tell the world how much we loved our mums, or how our dads had interfered with us ... even though before that moment we had no words, no apparent speech understanding, putting to one side the fact that no one had ever thought to teach us to read or write, what with the really severe disabilities and everything. It was as if, out of thin air we (not them) would magically discover this thing called language in a written form ... out of nowhere! As I say, I don't understand it, but other people do have some interesting ideas about us and how to treat us.

Or some of them would sometimes put really tight arm straps on some of us to stop us fiddling with ourselves, or whole jackets with buckles on the arms that went behind your back. Or they might put us in a room with no handle on the inside of the door and no windows to the outside. They might put us in there and not let us out, purely for our own good. To help us; to give us time to think about what we might have been doing.

To give us time to learn better behaviour in that room on our own.

And it certainly wasn't unusual just to take out all our teeth. That was a matter of routine, just in case we, well, I can only presume they were worried that one of us might try to eat one of them; so out with the teeth ... the lot. Well, we wouldn't want anyone to suffer ... not by getting a bit chewed on. We shouldn't put anyone at risk of any unnecessary suffering ... no, not at all.

Or sometimes they might prod us with a plugged-in stick to help us to learn to do something, or actually to learn to stop doing something, to help us to learn the right kinds of better behaviour. Or sometimes they might take it on themselves to inject small metal ball bearings into our heads ... or sometimes take some of the 'bad' bits of our brains away when we weren't looking or put small sticks inside the front of our heads and twist them around for a while to help us. Yes, they might try to help us in those ways, do those kinds of helpful things to us, to help us be more normal, more like them.

Or there were some people, some of them with white coats or dresses on, going around dolling out all kinds of different pills and potions. Yes, they were really quite popular, those pills and potions, lots and lots of them, almost everyone had to take something at some time. You can sometimes still see the ones who had the most of that kind of stuff, the stronger pills and potions, because nowadays for some of them, well their tongues tend to have a life of their own. There they now sit, those ones who had it worst, sitting quietly with their tongues constantly pushing up and out of their mouths, as if they are trying to escape, their tongues that is, out from the back of their mouths. There they sit, with their heads slowly nodding to and fro, and their bodies occasional quivering and jolting. All of this to help us.

Sorry about this. If I could put myself in your place, I could imagine that it's a bit uncomfortable to listen to what used to happen, all that kind of stuff behind closed doors, well actually behind big walls, and big heavy locked doors a lot of the time. Out of sight and out of mind. There is probably a joke in there somewhere, but it probably isn't the right time to be looking for a laugh, not now.

Luckily I can't remember any of it, not in any detail; how could I, with my non-memory, but there still linger faint shadows of my past, of such experiences, somewhere deep inside of me. I did most of my growing up in a big place, in a place with big walls and big locked doors. I lived in such a place for most of my life ... so there are still shadows that lurk deep inside me, in what I have of a memory. I know that they are there, I know that something is there, but luckily for me, I can't get at them ...

Perhaps that distance, the distance in time, and the big doors and walls helped hide these kinds of things, perhaps it allowed the ones with the strange ideas of how to help keep it going, away from others with prying eyes and questioning minds. It wasn't always clear who had the problem, whose behaviour needed changing, but it was always people like me that ended up having it done to them, whatever it was. No one tried to ask us, so we didn't have a say.

Unfortunately, some people like to think that they already know it all, how best to treat us, so they don't need to ask. They think that they have some special ideas that will help, some better way of thinking and seeing the world. And unfortunately, lots of other people seem to like the idea of other people having the ideas, to do that kind of heavy thinking for them. Perhaps it somehow removes the burden of thinking from them or lets them off the hook in some way. And perhaps somehow it is drilled into people to only accept big or difficult ideas from certain kinds of people. Unfortunately, that kind of 'go to' ideas person certainly isn't me, or anyone like me.

I am sure they all meant well; I am sure they all did … probably. And I am sure they were trying their best to help in what sometimes might seem to them like a bit of a hopeless task. So, you have to give them some credit for trying. But please remember, in future, if you try to be one of the people who care for me, try to think for yourself. Try to think what it would be like to be done to from my angle, down here in my chair, not a word I can say to comment on or change things. Nothing I can do to stop the putting in or taking out, the strapping in or holding down. Nothing I can say to say, "please don't".

Try to think what I might think about what you do to me, and people like me. I'm not saying it would be easy, but please promise me you would try.

'Love makes nonsense of space
and time will disappear
Love and logic keep us clear
Reason is on our side, love'

(U2: Miracle Drug)

It is one o'clock ... time for the news from the BBC ...

I hear that just about every day, or so it seems, and because of that I actually quite like it. Don't ask me why, or what it is about it, but somehow the words seem reassuring and friendly ... they have become a bit of a constant in my life. I haven't the faintest idea what the words mean, well what they might mean to other people, the ones who use the same sort of words when they talk, but to me it means that I am here, at home, with familiar things going on. It means that the world, well, it means that my world is okay, is untroubled by events, is undisturbed and as it should be.

To me those sounds mean that things are in their proper time and place, including me, and that the connections between things are still secure and working well. It means that the day, and thus my world more generally has some dependable framework or fabric that supports it, that my own day has some familiar threads running through it that hold it all together. That's what it says to me, and so I am glad to hear it.

I know that certain things will follow on from here, from this present moment. Yes, it's a kind of marker that is woven into the day by an unseen hand. Actually, it isn't its presence that really counts, although it does, it is really nice to hear the words when they come. No, it's actually the lack of their absence that is important; that would be felt much more strongly. If that sound, that marker, wasn't to come at some point in the day, if I didn't hear those words, then at some point I would start to feel a tiny bit different about things. I wouldn't know why, and I won't realise it straight away, but at some point I would notice that those familiar, time marking words had gone missing. That at some point in time, somewhere along the way, at some time in the day, the words had failed to come, that the fabric of the world was missing a little bit of something, that a little bit of the support structure of the day, of the world, had somehow been lost along the way … and then I wouldn't feel quite so, well, quite so okay about things.

Funny that really, the absence of something being more important, more powerful than its actual presence; something not being there, when expected, hitting home much harder than the thing itself. I wonder why that is … actually I don't, but it's interesting that the presence of those sounds, those words have as they float past me, have a habit-like no-effect on me. But if they didn't come, if they got lost for some reason, well then that would leave me, well, well out of sorts.

If I could, I'm sure that I would wonder what they are actually for, those words that is, what purpose they serve in the world. Am I the only one who feels this way about them?

Actually, things aren't quite as normal as they normally are at the moment, not these last few days. For some reason, and I don't know what it is, it's been a bit hectic around here. Everyone seems to be doing everything a bit more quickly than usual, upping their tempo, really getting on with stuff. Doing other stuff, for more of the time, often in other rooms. So, it somehow feels a bit different. There is a bit of a different quality to the way they, my staff people, have had with me, with being with me, a bit. Not ignoring, not dismissive, no, but not really being around me as much. Not being quite as interested, not quite spending as much time with me as they normally do. Well, not all of them, some more than others.

So, they seem extra busy, more preoccupied with moving stuff, other stuff, around the house, finding new places for some of the things, cleaning up behind things, and under them, sorting piles of papery things, looking for things they haven't seen for months. Yes, it's been about them wanting to look at and do other stuff, and not look at and do as much stuff with me. I don't think so, it's just a feeling I have, but I'm good on having feelings.

This has happened before, and then some unusual people come around to see these things, this other stuff, to see where they have been put, and to see if it is clean behind and under where they have been put, the things that is. To be fair, they sometimes also have a look at me, and say some things to me, but not for too long. Then they go back to looking around, going in and out of all rooms, and saying a lot of things to the staff people. I don't know these people. I don't know who they are or where they come from.

To be honest, I don't really know what to make of them, and I'm not sure what they make of me. I don't know what they are really looking for, and whether they are really looking at me, to see how I am and what I do. Perhaps they trying to be friends with me, and don't really know how to. Perhaps they are trying to be friends with the staff people. When they look at me I hope I seem okay to them. I hope they get a good impression of me, although they don't stay that long, not nearly long enough to have a really good look at me, a proper look, to get to know me, to get to know who I am and what I can do. Perhaps they'll come back; they often do.

Perhaps they are looking to see if I'm happy, or if I'm sad, or whether they like me, or if I might like them. Perhaps they're looking for something, something that they've lost. Yes, maybe they're looking to find something; perhaps a something, or a person, or an old friend? But like I say, I don't really know what they are looking for. Perhaps whatever it is they're looking for is always here when they aren't, which is almost all the time.

But when they are here, looking for whatever it is they are looking for, it seems to make everyone feel a bit uncomfortable. Perhaps it's something that they say, but everyone seems to get on edge, including me. I can sense it in my staff people, they suddenly seem to have less time, and less of a mind to give much time to me. Their minds seem absorbed with the other stuff, with the other things, and we start to come a bit second, a bit.

Yes, they do a little less with me, spend a little less time with me, and when they do I feel like they are not there as much as usually, not being as present with me, if that makes sense to you. It's as if everyone has only half an eye on me, and half an eye looking back over their shoulders. Not really, but it feels like that. Looking out for something they have missed, something they might have forgotten, or forgotten to do, or forgotten not to do.

They seem a bit unsettled, a bit distant with their own thoughts and feelings, and I get to feel a bit of that as well. Yes, I sense a bit of anxiety in them. I know the feeling myself. It's a kind of anxiousness you get when you don't know why, you just sense it, the sort that creeps up on you. It's like you are expecting something unfamiliar, and possibly something not too good, to happen. It's not nice, feeling like that, and for no real reason. Well, no reason that you know of, or I know of when I get it, just some kind of expecting of something not in your control to happen.

I get that as well. I don't know why, but I can pick it up from other people, from those around me. I sense their anxiousness and become anxious as well. I've no idea why, but its real. It somehow comes across in waves from other people, unseen, unheard, unwelcome. And then it slowly builds up in me, the feeling at some point being strong enough to break through, even though it doesn't have any real cause, well, not one I know of. Perhaps you get it too, that anxiety passed on from others. Perhaps you sense it, and then catch it from others. People eh, aren't we strange, strange kinds of things, at times, I suppose.

Maybe it's just some of us. Perhaps just some of us are more prey to these kinds of feelings than others, anxiousness and the like, whether it's their own or passed on from others. Although actually some people, some of my people, don't seem to suffer too much. Some of them just get on as before, seemingly unaffected by all the extra busyness going on around them. Although, and I don't mean anything by it, but these ones seem to be the ones who don't normally do a great deal anyway. They seem to be the ones who always go at their own pace. You have to admire them, don't you, well to a certain extent. They go on being okay with what they do, satisfied that what they do is more or less the right thing, seemingly confident that they do more or less enough of more or less the right sort of thing.

And confidence is generally a good thing, I think (probably). A quality to be admired. Although it's not really a quality I would associate with myself. No, confidence is something I seek in others, especially those that care for me, to know what to do and do it well, without nervous hands and voices. I need that confidence, which can also come out in waves from others. That's good that, that passed on feeling of confidence, from those that take responsibility for me, for us. Yes, then I like confidence; confident, reassuring movements, confident, reassuring sounds, confident, reassuring holding and touching. Yes, that's good that is. Then I feel confident things are going to be okay.

Although actually you don't want too much confidence getting into the wrong hands, into the hands of people who don't know the best ways to care for me, for people like us. That's when it can do a lot of damage. Actually, it can be a lethal combination, a combination of too little understanding combined with too much self-belief. That's when things can go badly wrong. It's only been some, some staff, but it was those staff who were over-confident with the feeding, confidently shovelling in with the spoons. That's when it can be a problem, them 'knowing' what they are doing, and doing it wrong.

That's a bad combination, those who do it wrong but don't sense that what they're doing just isn't right. Those who can't hear or won't listen. Those who can't see or won't be shown. When they have confidence, too much of it, and when they know their own mind and just carry on regardless, well, believe me, that's when things can go oh so badly wrong.

`When you have so much time to spend on so very little ...'

When you have so much time to spend on so very little, on the very little you can actually, actively do, when so little is asked or expected of you, you often find yourself getting more and more fixated on things, on certain objects or sensations.

When you have so much time, well, then you have the time to do it, to get really into something you see; to get really focused on something. And for someone like me, when you spend a lot of time not really involved with something outside of yourself, then there is very little else effectively competing for your attention. So, because you spend a lot of time like this, you become very well practised at focusing in on things, right in on the minute details of the things. You can do this with anything, focusing in on anything you have at your disposal, whether these are real things or just your own physical feelings or inner sensations.

Actually, it doesn't really matter whether the thing or the feeling you are focusing in on is exactly the same as the last time, the last time you focused in on it. But if it is, then that's good, that's reassuring, that's how you really want it to be, that's what you'd hope for. Deep down that's what you really want. Well, it is for me, it being and feeling the same as before. That's reassuring, knowing what I know, and having that confirmed. That's good, that's okay, that's how it should be, things the same, things being what they should be, things knowing how to be and how to feel. Yes, I like that, feeling the same as before, like my chair strap, or the buckle, there just for me, always available, allowing me access.

And once you've focused in on it, on the thing, on the chair strap or the buckle, felt it's feeling, sensed its sensation, well then, if you are in the right mood, and there's nothing else out there of interest going on, then it can just keep going. Once you're in the moment with this kind of inner focusing in, keeping the outside world at bay, well then it can be really hard to stop. It draws you in and hooks you. The end of doing it is the same as the start of doing it, and you no longer know which is which. From the start to the end, to the start to the end in a continuing loop around itself. And you forget when and why you even started.

It's as if you constantly need to check it, the thing, the sensation, is still the same, the same as this time, and the time just gone, even while you're actually still doing it. And so it starts again, back from the start (where else), just to check if it is still the same. To reassure yourself that it's as it was the last time, and the time before, and the time before that. Then you're caught in the flow, a flow of checking and rechecking and giving it everything, giving it everything you can in terms of your attention and you're looking and feeling and sometimes listening, really zoning in on it, blocking everything else out so that you can really tell if it is still right, or not.

And then if it isn't somehow quite right, although generally it usually is, but if it is somehow a tiny bit different, say the chair strap or the buckle, then you want to know, you want to be sure of the details of this change, however slight. Actually, then you need to know how it's a bit different, what has changed, how exactly does it feel different from before. So, you refocus in on it again, the chair strap or the buckle, back to the start, over and over again, time disappearing in a closed loop of internal sensations.

And perhaps this slightly different thing or feeling or sensation is now going to become the normal thing, the way it is always going to be from now on. So, then you have to go back to the start and check again, to see if the thing or feeling or sensation is now the same, the same as it has now become, but a bit different from how it used to be, different but now the same different thing, even if only slightly. Yes, it can get quite complicated. It can often take a lot this kind of checking and rechecking. So, you need to be really thorough. You can never relax and leave these types of things unattended; they might change at any time, you need to keep on checking, just in case.

For me it can get like that with the belt strap buckle. Its' here at my shoulder, that strap and the buckle. They are always there when I am here in my chair, they are like constant companions, and they tend to remain very much the same, almost all the time, in that way they are really reliable, and that is nice. But still, it doesn't stop me from checking it, just in case, lots of times, over and over again, just to see, just to check. My thing is that I tend to run my chin over it, slowly up and down, just to check that it feels the same, hard and smooth and buckle shaped and buckle sized, and with that side bit, with its bit of a raised edge, just there, just there, there it is. Just there, just where it should be, just there again. No, yes, it hasn't moved. Ye, no, it isn't any different. There it is, same as before, just where it normally is, right at the right point as I rub my chin slowly over it, constant and reassuring, not different, just the same.

But what if, sometime, when I'm not checking it, it was to become somehow a bit different, what then? So, I better just check again, just in case, and yes, yes, it isn't any different, and no, no, it is just the same, with the raised bit, just as it should be, that's okay then.

Well, it's okay for now, I can relax, just for a while knowing it is okay, okay and the same, just as it should be, just the same. I might have mentioned I like familiarity, so it's nice to know, that it still has its sameness, its constancy, and that's a good feeling. Because you never know, it could change. It might be different next time, so when I have the time, like now, then it's good to check it, it keeps me feeling okay, feeling attached to the thing, the buckle. I feel a bit like a part of it, or it of me, we've become a bit attached, less separate, less distinct.

We've become part of the same thing or the same activity, or both, the buckle and me, me and the buckle. Me rubbing it, it being rubbed, chin to buckle, buckle to chin, rubbing together, the buckle rubbing my chin, my chin rubbing the buckle. While I'm doing it, while I'm in the buckle rubbing zone, while I'm in the flow of the rubbing activity, it's hard to say which it is, which way around, who or what is being rubbed and who or what is doing the rubbing. It's just there, I'm just there, with the buckle, doing it all together, round and round and round again, checking and being checked, the activity building up its own momentum, the flow of the activity taking me along with it, from start to finish to start again.

Once you are in there, in the zone, right in the midst of it, the rubbing, the being rubbed, then it's hard to get back out. It's hard to bring yourself out and round. I'm not the worst at that, getting stuck in the flow of an activity. I'm not the worst by far, but I can feel myself slipping into the flow, being swept along by it. Once in that focused and timeless zone it's hard to get back out, it's hard to let it go. It's hard to break out of it even when the rubbing starts to damage me, even when the skin starts to break down and open up, even then it's hard to break out. You can't see or feel where the end of it is. There isn't a point to break out from as the end is lost in amongst all the starts. And anyway, stopping feels like you may have to give something up, something important. You can't take the risk and leave yourself open to something that feels uncertain.

It's the not knowing, it's the not being sure, that's not easy. So, just one more check, just one more rub, you see if it might have changed since I was last looking, or feeling, or rubbing. You never know, it might have chosen its moment, knowing my attention was elsewhere, knowing it wasn't being attended to, that's when it's bound to change. I feel inside that it will change, at some time, when I least expect it. That's when it will change. That's when I expect something to happen. So, I better just rub it again, just to make sure, chin, buckle, buckle, chin, here I go again, back in the zone, back going with the flow.

Perhaps the buckle feels the same way about me and my chin, perhaps that's why it's always there. Perhaps it is just checking that my chin feels the same, perhaps it just wants to be reassured that my chin isn't somehow different. Perhaps it gets worried, I know I do. Or perhaps it stays the same because it knows that that is how I like it, that that is what I seek from it, sameness and not difference, so perhaps it does its job well, perhaps it stays the same on purpose. Or perhaps it's like me in that it doesn't have enough to do, to fill its time. So perhaps it gets stuck in the flow of the activity of checking my chin to see if it has stayed the same and then also gets lost in the flow of it all, just like me. Perhaps? Who knows? … not me, not you, and probably not even the buckle. The buckle certainly has many qualities, I can testify to that, but knowing why it does the chin rubbing probably isn't one of them.

Yes, this particular buckle certainly has many qualities: it is reliable, there where it should be, doing its buckling; it is reassuring, with its familiar sameness, with its sticky out edge; and most importantly, it is there for me to check. You might say it's just a buckle, but it's my buckle, my special buckle, the buckle that is always there, on my chair, in its place, as it should be, with its special edge, my special buckle … let's just hope it stays that way.

Wait on a bit, now there's something going on …

Wait on a bit, now there's something going on, and it's not the buckle. There is something being said, from outside, something being said to me, some sounds, some words as you would call them …

> *"Twas brillig, and the slithy toves*
> *Did gyre and gimble in the wabe:*
> *All mimsy were the borogoves,*
> *And the mome raths outgrabe."*

Yep, that's what the sound sounded like, that's what it said. To be honest, although I don't know what it means, or what it's meant to mean, I know it somehow sounds interesting. It's happened before. It comes from this man. He comes to sit close up next to me, quite often nowadays, and he likes to say this kind of stuff to me. And I'm sure it is for me. However, I have to admit that it doesn't mean a blind thing to me, not a thing, no change there then, but … but I like the rhythm of it though. I do like it. I get something pleasurable from hearing it.

The sound bobbles and bobs along nicely, dipping down and bobbing up. It's almost as if the rhythm and the shape of the sounds carries some special kind of meaning, like words I suppose, which obviously I don't understand. But somehow it doesn't seem to matter that it's nonsense to me, I still like to hear it.

Perhaps that's how it's meant to be, with these particular nicely bobbing and babbling sounds. They're different to the normal talking sounds that people mainly do around me and to me. They seem nice in themselves just as sounds, nothing more than that, sounding nice on the ear, and perhaps that's meant to be the point. So, the not making any sense, that doesn't really matter with these sounds, not to me. I can hear them just for the sake, nothing more, sounds that are nice just for the sake of being sounds. You might not hear them like that. For you the meaning is probably crystal clear, but for me, well, with these sounds I just like their feel, the way they play on my ears.

And this guy really seems to enjoy doing it, I can tell that from the sounds he makes; not the form or shape of the sounds, but from the tone he uses. He gives it some real gusto as he says it to me out of a book. He seems to really get some pleasure from saying it out loud to me. So, we both get something good out of it, each as one, both together ...

> *"Beware the Jabberwock, my son!*
> *The jaws that bite, the claws that catch!*
> *Beware the Jubjub bird and shun*
> *The frumious Bandersnatch!"*

Oooh, it all sounds a bit scary, but not too scary. The sounds seem to be nicely exciting in a way I can cope with, so I can get a bit excited without having to do anything at all scary. So, it somehow feels nicely secure, and a little bit scary, both at the same time. Yes, both a tad exciting and reassuring familiar, both running along rhythmically as one, together. Oh, here he goes again ...

> *"He took his vorpal sword in hand:*
> *Long time the manxome foe he sought --*
> *So rested he by the Tumtum tree,*
> *And stood awhile in thought.*

> *And, as in uffish thought he stood,*
> *The Jabberwock, with eyes of flame,*
> *Came whiffling through the tulgey wood,*
> *And burbled as it came!"*

Blimey, it's building up a bit now, to what I don't know, but I sense there is something exciting happening in the tone of this guy's voice. It's getting a bit faster and louder and a tiny bit higher, even his breathing is getting shorter and shallower. It sounds like something is about to happen. Well, not really happen, but sort of happen, because I can sense it in sounds. Something is building, building up to something …

> *"One, two! One, two! And through and through*
> *The vorpal blade went snicker-snack!*
> *He left it dead, and with its head*
> *He went galumphing back.*
>
> *And, has thou slain the Jabberwock?*
> *Come to my arms, my beamish boy!*
> *O frabjous day! Callooh! Callay!'*
> *He chortled in his joy."*

That sense of something is still there in the sounds, in the words that carry no meaning for me. If only I could nail it down, actually put my finger on what is actually happening, what it all means that is. All that language and wordy stuff. Stuff, words that is, that people like you use to make yourselves and your meaning clear. You seem to spend so much time doing it that I can only presume that you're really good at it, using words like these to make yourself really clear.

Or perhaps not, perhaps you spend so much time doing it because it isn't very clear, and you need to keep going over it, making it better. Making sure other people know what it is you're on about, helping them find the meaning hiding somewhere in amongst it all. Unfortunately, it's all well beyond me, although I would take a bet that I have almost certainly spent quite a bit of time *burbling* and *whiffling* at some point in the past, I must have done, surely. And anyway, he's cracking on again, and just like me with my strap, he's gone right back to the start ...

> *"Twas brillig, and the slithy toves*
> *Did gyre and gimble in the wabe:*
> *All mimsy were the borogoves,*
> *And the mome raths outgrabe."*

So, like so often, I don't know if something is starting or it's ending, setting going or coming to stop. And it doesn't matter really, I like the sounds, even if to me they are a load of old nonsense. So, to me it doesn't really matter if he starts at the start and ends at the end, or if he starts at the end and ends at the start. I don't mind as the sounds are nice either way round. Mind you, for all I know he might be reading it backwards, and do you know what, well, I wouldn't mind one bit; so long as its rhythmical and musical tone was there. Then that's okay with me.

I could hear it many times over though. Yes, why not do it all over again? Just the same as before, whether it be backwards or forwards. Remember I like the familiar, I like a bit of repetition. It is what I am used to after all. I know what I like, and I do, honestly, know what I like. Oh, and I also generally like what I know; lots of what I know.

Although actually I don't mind some odd bits of variety, so long as it's quite like what I know and like, and like and know already. Yes, I'm okay with that kind of variety, when it's not too different, only a bit different, but mainly the same. That'll do fine thanks.

This chap, this man, he reads other stuff to me as well. He seems to have a list of regular favourites that he reads to me, and I like most of them. They've somehow grown on me, both him and the sounds he makes. I really like another one that makes him sound like he is actually moving. When he reads it, it makes me feel as if I'm going with him, but staying still, both at the same time ...

> *"This is the Night Mail crossing the border,*
> *Bringing the cheque and the postal order,*
> *Letters for the rich, letters for the poor,*
> *The shop at the corner and the girl next door.*
> *Pulling up Beattock, a steady climb:*
> *The gradient's against her, but she's on time.*
> *Past cotton-grass and moorland boulder*
> *Shovelling white steam over her shoulder"*

Yes, I like that one as well. To me it goes: "da-da-da-da-da, da-da-da-da, da-da-da-da-da, da-da-da-da". It just tootles along, the sounds that is, and it feels right. The sounds he makes fit the all the "da-da-da-da-da-ing", and he also taps it out onto my chair as some kind of sensory physical accompaniment, as he goes along. Ta-ta-ta-ta-ta, ta-ta-ta-ta, ta-ta-ta-ta-ta, ta-ta-ta-ta, tapping gently onto my chair; ta-ta-ta-ta, ta-ta-ta-ta-ta, ta-ta-ta-ta, in time with his sounds, moving it along nicely.

All that ta-ta-ta-ta-ta-ing just makes the sense of it all the more real, all the more absorbing, all the more as if we are both there together, experiencing whatever it is, together. Yes, I like it, don't ask me why, but I do, and so does he …

> *"Letters of thanks, letters from banks,*
> *Letters of joy from the girl and the boy,*
> *Receipted bills and invitations*
> *To inspect new stock or visit relations…*
>
> *The chatty, the catty, the boring, adoring,*
> *The cold and official and the heart's outpouring*
>
> *Clever, stupid, short and long,*
> *The typed and the printed and the spelt all wrong"*

Yes, I do like that one as well. I can just sit here, with this bloke, and have some kind of experience without doing anything or going anywhere. Having a sense of something without actually moving outside; but feeling outside of myself. And all that from the stuff he says to me that I don't understand. Not bad that. That makes a nice change, with the sounds being nice and shared with me in a way that brings us both together, giving us both some pleasure, both of us getting some sense of a sensation in a way that we can both actually share. Somehow communicating about something that seems special, but which is at the same time unclear in what it actually is or says. Knowing that it is somehow really important, even though for me I haven't the slightest clue what it is that he's going on about. Maybe you get that same sensation? I hope so, I thinks it's really nice.

This bloke, he's still here by the way ...

This bloke, he's still here by the way. He not only reads and says funny stuff to me, stuff in words I don't understand, but he also makes my noises back to me. Yes, he makes the sounds I make myself, back to me: my breathing, my huffing and puffing sounds, any sounds I make, then so does he; right back to me, right up close, right in near my face, so close that I can actually feel his breath on my cheeks. And I like that, I really like that.

You see, when he does this, when he makes my sounds, the sounds he makes are generally just right, just the right sounds for me, and just right for how I'm feeling at the time I'm making the sounds. So yes, I really like it when he does them back to me; from me to him, to me, to him, together between each other. It's as if the sounds I make have some real meaning for him, because he seems to get some meaning out of them. I can tell by his tone, he seems to understand something in my sounds, and then he does them back to me. Not always exactly the same, no, sometimes a bit different, but always with a smiling sound or a laugh at the end. And sometimes he stretches them out, and sometimes he whispers them back in my ears, and sometimes he says them loudly and excitedly.

When he does this, when he echoes my sounds, when he sounds like me, then I tend to give him some more to do, and then we are both doing it, speaking my words, talking in my

127

language, doing it in my way, Harry's way. Sometimes he does it at the same time as me and sometimes we take turns, sometimes we get louder and sometimes we get quieter, but always we end up really tuning in to each other, getting closer and communicating better.

And not just with the sounds. Sometimes he kind of rhythmical touches me. Sometimes he will gently rub up and down my arms, slowly and gently, and he does that with a really nice kind of rhythm. He actually uses my rhythm, Harry's rhythm, the one I use to breathe with. He kind of matches that and rubs me along with it, and somehow it seems to match my mood, the rubbing does. Sometimes when I am excited and my breathing is excited, so his rubbing seems to know this, and he rubs me at just the right excited speed. And if I'm a bit tired or feeling a bit chilled, then he rubs me in a relaxing or chilled way, his rubbing seems to know how to rub to match how I feel. That's clever rubbing, it really is a clever kind of rubbing.

Sometimes he gets really close in and looks me right in my eyes, one or the other, right there, right in front of my face. Wow. And it makes me look him back in the eye, because he's there, right close up, but at least I can see him really clearly there, any further back and I can't really focus on him, or anything really, so he gets really close in, and sometimes makes some sounds, and looks me straight in the eye. Then I can look straight back at him, in the eye, and then I can focus a bit more, for a bit longer, and I know he is saying something important to me with his eyes. He is telling me something about himself, and about me, about us both by looking at me so straight in the eye, and so intensely. No one else does this this way, no one else really gets in this close for this long, and I think that that means something.

I can feel it, the thing he is telling me, I can feel it in my feelings, not really in my head, but more all over. I can feel something like significance, it's a weird feeling if you don't get it much, feeling significant. It's nice, yes, I like it. But I'm not really sure either why or how. This significance, well it's nice, but not like being warm is nice, or being tickled is nice, or feeling full is nice, but it's a nice feeling none the less.

It's one of the feelings I like to feel best. Actually, I have quite a few feelings, not just the physical sort I feel in my body. I have other feelings that I feel deep down inside me, feelings like contentment, or surprise, or uneasiness, or irritation. Sometimes, if I'm in the right mood, I have feelings of mild amusement or even intense fun. And for me my feelings are just as important as I guess they are to you, it's just that I can't label them with words, make them into thoughts and say them out loud.

And anyway, if we can, perhaps we should ask ourselves where do these thought things come from anyway; mainly from feelings I guess, mostly, probably … well possibly. Yes, actually, maybe they do. Who knows? Certainly I don't, I can't. But feelings and thoughts, both in there at the same time, both coming from somewhere inside, somewhere deeper down, somewhere inaccessible, out of sight, out of reach, but not out of mind.

But they do come up, come out from somewhere. They do tend to surface at some point, these feelings; well, they do for me. Perhaps because you have words, words you can use to build your thoughts with, perhaps for you they will go together, thoughts and feelings. Perhaps sometimes one, perhaps sometimes the other, perhaps sometimes both together. Perhaps for you they might come one after the other, one following the lead of other, sometimes a feeling, and then a thought, sometimes a thought and then a feeling (although not for me remember, I just get the non-wordy feelings).

But even if it is only feelings, they are my feelings, feelings without thoughts. Sometimes they surface quite suddenly, like a strong and unforeseen urge just to do something. Suddenly an urge emerging into a real feeling; an urge to move, an urge to shout out, an urge to shut my eyes. I certainly get urges, and they come from somewhere. Perhaps urges come from the same place as feelings, and even thoughts perhaps. In there and down there, out of sight, waiting to appear, waiting for their opportunity to jump up and out into the daylight of our minds as fully fledged impulses, or fully fashioned feelings, or fully formed thoughts; perhaps they're really all one and the same. Urges, feelings, thoughts, being born into awareness or action, often coming up uninvited. What's that about then? Where is that place, and what's going on there? Who knows? Not me, that's for sure.

I also have general feelings that tend to be with me all the time. General feelings towards things, general feelings about things. Perhaps it's a bit like you would hold general thoughts about things, not just occasional thoughts about things, but steady reliable opinions about things. Well, I have general feelings about things, feelings about familiar things that I am familiar with, and I especially have general feelings about myself, and about who I am and what I can and can't do. Perhaps these would count as opinions? Perhaps, opinions, or feelings, or thoughts, or does it really matter what you call them? But I don't generally have a steady or overall feeling of me being somehow significant, about there being some general significance about me out there somewhere in the world; not much anyway. So, it is nice when I occasionally do, like now, with this bloke getting in close, making contact with me, making my sounds, looking me in the eyes.

Anyway, back to this bloke, the one who brings along me some of my significance with him. Sometimes when he gets really close in, he plays some kind of game with me, a close-in eye contact game. He looks in at me and then quickly looks away, letting me find his eyes with mine, and then blinking them shut, just to open them really wide moments later. I like it, well I think I do. I like how he does it in a way that doesn't have too many moments in it. Not too many moments for me to lose interest; just enough for me to notice and then wait, to feel a sense of something building, something like suspense and expectation.

Again, I don't know why he does it, but I can't really fault him for it. And don't ask me why it works, or why it works every time, it just does. It seems right, there is significance in there, yes, somewhere. But also, there is something like fun in there. It just feels like fun, and therefore actually it is fun. Yes, I sense that there is fun out there in the world, and some of it is for me. So actually yes, fun is another feeling I sometimes get, and I get it when he does this intense looking thing. And not just for me, I get it for both of us ... both fun and significance, for both of us, both at the same time, it emerging and running between us; from him to me, from me to him, both at the same time.

And that's not all. Sometimes this bloke, he brings some things with him, things he helps me to hold or explore, to sense and or feel. Sometimes we might play games with the things, shaking them or pulling and pushing them one way and then the other, battling a bit for control. Some of the things make noises, or feel funny, buzzing or humming away to themselves. Some even make their own light; flashing away when you tip them up or over.

Yes, some things, some of these things he brings can be really interesting. I'm not sure what they're all for, apart from being for me when I feel or sense them. There are some soft things, some hard things, some things with different shapes and feels to the outside of them. Sometimes these things go up against me, sometimes they are put into my hands, sometimes they are waved in front of me. All with their own characteristics, all feeling different, all looking different, some even sounding different. All these things, this other stuff, coming from out there. These things, they come in and out of my life, sometimes there, sometimes not, sometimes touching me, sometimes not, sometime under me, sometimes on top of me.

It might be interesting to know where they all come from, whose they are, and what they're really for. Although actually I really don't care. It isn't a question I ever really trouble myself with. But come they do, somehow, from somewhere, from somewhere that isn't here.

Actually, in my life I've encountered loads of things, things that come from somewhere out there. Sometimes for a short while, sometimes for much longer. Things that move, things that move me. Big things, small things, heavy and light, things that go on me, things that go under me, and sometimes things that go in me. Some of these things I get to see, some things I only get to feel; feel on me, up me, or in me. Things that are soft and things that aren't, things with a bit of give, things that don't give an inch.

Everywhere there are things. I suppose, possibly some of them are mine, possibly. If I had a better sense of ownership I might have an opinion, or a general feeling about that, about whether some of the things are mine or not, like the things that come along with this bloke. But really, I don't really know. But some of them I do like better than others, the ones that feel and act nice, the things that are familiar as well, those are the ones I like the best. If they feel, and smell nice, and are nice and familiar, then I like them; I hope those things are mine. But some of those other things, no, not really. I don't really have any positive feelings towards those others, those 'in' me or 'up' me kind of things. I don't really like them, what's their game then, eh? What are they up to when they're in or up me? That's not very nice is it, for a thing to do that, the in and the up things. No, I don't like them.

To be honest, I'm not really very good at knowing about many different things. Actually, that's an understatement, for me either things are the things I already know, or they are pretty suspect to me. I need quite a bit of time to get to know new things, to sense if they are going to be okay with me. It takes me a long time to categorise new things alongside my sense of my familiar okay things. I can't really use the idea of things being similar to something else to get a good sense of things.

So, yes, I like things to be really nearly exactly the same as something else, so alike that I can't tell them apart, or else to me they are completely different. It's very black or white with me and things; there doesn't seem to be much of an in-between with things for me. Things tend to be either one thing, or a completely different thing. So, for me there aren't things that are 'a bit like' other things, a bit similar. If they aren't the same, then they are completely different.

A bit alike? No, that's no use to me, things are either one thing or they are something else entirely. A bit similar? No, the idea of something being a bit similar is no use to me. Its either the same or different, that's all I need to know about things. This or that, known or unknown, those kinds of categories will do for me, they will have to, it's all I can manage. So, let's keep stuff simple and straightforward. With things, yes, let's keep them very much the same, mainly.

It's difficult for me with things. I can't really describe them, I can't give them names or labels, and I struggle to put them into what you would call categories. They are just what they are, a jumble of features or such like. It's the features or characteristics that I tend to recognise, the features of the things, not the things themselves, not unless they are really very, very familiar. It's the feel and the smell and the sight of it, the thing, that goes to make it up as a thing.

Because I don't know what many things are for, or what they do, or where they've come from, then mostly I can't properly sort them out. To put things together in my mind as this 'sort' of thing or that 'sort' of thing. So, I have no choice really, mostly, I have to go with the jumble of features or characteristics, the things that are there in the nature of it. Not the type of thing it is overall, but the jumble of things that go to make up the thing that might help me to recognise it, as a certain sort of that thing. So that tends to make life quite difficult, this not being able to sort things out.

Interestingly, well I hope interestingly (to you), like I've mentioned before, the absence of things can be more significant to me than their presence. When things are there, in their right place, that's fine, they seem to properly exist, sometimes even as proper things (not just as a jumble of features), there and just getting on with being there, not drawing attention to themselves, not making a fuss about being there. But when they should be there but aren't, when they have deserted their post, not there when and where they should be, well that's a different matter. That can be really unnerving, especially if I didn't see them go, if they're no longer making themselves available to me to be seen or smelt or touched, that's when they kind of announce their former presence by not being there where you expect them. Its then that some things can become more real, more noticeable than if they were still there. They kind of shout out: I'm not here anymore, I'm not where I should be, where you were expecting me! That's sometimes when you really notice things the most, when they have disappeared without letting you know. Aren't things funny sometimes, especially when they're not there. Yes, it can come as a shock, especially when familiar things are not there. Yes, sometimes when things are so familiar that I can recognise them as things, sometimes even my things, when they aren't there, when they're gone, that's the hardest bit to understand. Where have they gone? Will they come back?

It would be useful to know more about things, things that are there, and things that aren't, things that sometimes are and sometimes aren't there without telling you. Yes, I would like to know more about things; what do all these things do? where do they go? what are they for?

Yes, that would be interesting. There's power in that kind of knowing; power over things. If only I could know them better, better describe them, sort them out better. If only I could think more about them, know what they're for and what they're up to (especially if they're wanting to get up me) then I think their power over me, their power to do things to me wouldn't be so bad. Maybe, perhaps?

'The songs are in your eyes
I see them when you smile
I've had enough of romantic love
I'd give it up, yeah, I'd give it up
For a Miracle Drug, a Miracle Drug
A Miracle Drug'

(U2: Miracle Drug)

Have you ever really thought about things?

I know I'm banging on about things, over and over a bit. But now I'm in the flow now about things (and remember how I struggle to break out from repetitions of doing things). But have you ever really thought about things? I mean really, really thought about just how something comes to be a thing? And have you ever really wondered about how you know something is a thing, a thing on its own, something that you know as a thing?

Do you ever wonder what separates one thing from another? Whether a collection of features grouped together automatically just becomes a thing? Is that what it is – or is there more to it than that? Does a certain group of similar minded smaller things jointly agree to come together and create some other, bigger or more complicated thing? A new thing on its own, something real, a single real new thing in the real world? Or is it just something we do in our heads? Putting these smaller things together? Perhaps they leave us to do all that kind of hard describing and labelling work, the things.

And also, how do some things become the same as other things when they are separate? Do they know that? Do they know that they are the same as all the other things that are the same as them? Do they care? It makes me wonder if a thing is just a thing that sits there all empty and lifeless, or does somehow it contain a sense of what it is, some essence of itself that radiates out all these sensations for us to feel and see and hear? Like the TV thing in the corner? A thing with its noises and colours and movements, drawing the staff people to look at it, and sometimes laugh or shout at it. Is that still the same thing when it's empty and lifeless, or has it become something else? I wonder what it prefers to be.

But I suppose, does any of it really matter? Does anyone really care? Outside of this, outside of these words, outside of this book thing, I certainly don't. But perhaps the things do? Perhaps they really do care? Yes, it is probably really important to them, otherwise why would they have bothered becoming what they are?

'And now it's time for Pointless'

Here we go again. It's on, the telly thing, it's doing its stuff, stuff that I recognise and apparently its saying that *'It's now time for Pointless'*. There's the familiar sounds and lights and movements, all together as a thing that I sort of recognise. Yes, I know that it is a thing, the telly, but this *'Pointless'* thing. Well, I'm not sure about that. Is that a part of it, the telly? Or a different other thing inside it? Again, I'm afraid I can't help you there. A different kind of thing within another thing, what's that about.

And this *'Pointless'* thing, well explain that to me if you can. Exactly the same sounds and movements on it, every time it's on. But it makes a nice marker in the day for me. Its so the same that its reassuringly familiar. I know where I am in the day as I know that some of the day has gone, quite a big part, and that there is some left to go, still quite a bit. So, in that sense it's really quite useful, a familiar and timely landmark, pointing out where we are in a day. I like that, but the rest of it, the *'Pointless'* thing, well I can't make anything from it, sense any point at all in it. But it's exactly the same every day, so I suppose that's the point, just something to mark and fill time during the day.

Oh-ho, here we go, I'm moving now. Something reassuring has been said to me, and then there's a reassuring touch to my arm, and I'm away, moving out of the telly room. Ahh, yes, I think I'm going down to the 'sensory' room now for a while. That *'Pointless'* thing must have finished doing what it does. I'm usually taken down here and put in this room at some point in the day. It's the room where they always play a special type of music, it's kind of a non-music music, it kind of comes and goes, without ever getting anywhere. It moves in and out your ears without ever staying there. It's the kind of music that you can never quite remember how it goes, it just goes. I don't mind it, and actually there is something quite nice about it. It's quite relaxing I suppose, which is okay at times, although not all the time. it's kind of stimulating, but not too much. It kind of sounds familiar without being memorable.

And then they put on some flickery, spangley lights. Lights in the ceiling, which flicker and fade in and out. And that's quite nice and relaxing as well. It's kind of like the music, a bit stimulating, but not too much. It kind of draws you out of yourself to look at them, shiny circles of light on the ceiling, the colours mixing together in and out, coming together and then moving apart. And then listening to the non-music music sounds that fill up the space all around, and then … then … well, to be honest I tend to shut my eyes and fall asleep.

I don't think I'm supposed to, but I can't help it. Although perhaps I am, but it just that I'm not being put to bed to do some proper sleeping. It's just that it all washes over me, like an overwhelming tide of tiredness, my eyes getting heavy and I'm powerless to resist it. Here I sit, sat in my chair trying to hold myself back from the irresistible song of sleepiness. It always wins, and I can't do anything other than accept the inevitable. Okay, I'll just go along with you, with this inner call to sleep, just for a minute. Okay, I'm all yours, I'm letting myself be submerged by it, by the lovely waves of lethargy. Yes, I'm all yours … I know I shouldn't … but … but … ahhhhhh …

I'm not really that lazy, not all the time

Don't get me wrong here, I'm not really that lazy, not all the time. I don't just sit my chair falling asleep. No, sometimes I do other, more active things, things that get me going physically, things that get me going in my head, things that get me going with my physical body feelings, and even at times things that get me moving more than I normally can when in my chair.

Sometimes I get to go to out to a big pool of lovely warm water. Not here in the house, not my normal bath, no, a pool that is much, much bigger. This place is somewhere else that I have to travel to in our minibus. When I get there and they pull and push me into my pool clothes, which for some reason doesn't fully cover me, but we'll let that ride. Well, in this big pool place I get lifted by a machine down into the lovely warm water. Not in on my own. No, of course not. No, when I'm in the water

I'm held there by some nice warm people. As I'm lowered in, slowly but surely the warm water seeps in and around me. And then it works its wonders. It really helps to loosen up my joints, to free up my tight and twisted arms and legs, just a bit.

Being moved about in a lovely warm pool by lovely warm people helps me move a bit easier, and it is lovely and warm. But it's not just the water, with its lovely warm wetness, its people in there with me, the warm women and men, there supporting me, holding me up, nice and secure. They hold me tight so that I don't tilt too much to one side or the other, so that I don't go under and breathe any of it in. Yes, I really like that as well, them holding me tight, and the lovely physical feel of the warm men and women; I have to say, for me, especially some of the women. Somehow, and I don't know exactly how, but they seem a bit physically warmer, somehow physically softer and so nicer to be held by. Yes, somehow more warm, somehow more soft, somehow even more floaty.

Perhaps I shouldn't say too much more here, I don't want to be misunderstood. I don't want people to think the worst of me, to think I have something not quite right in mind. But I do like physical contact, and after all, I am also a man. I have some deep physical feelings, and I can sense the difference. So, I do prefer the women to support me in the pool. I just do. You'll have to make of that what you will. I know what I like, and I like the bigger, softer, floatier woman to share my big pool sessions with. There it is, out in the open; although I can't be choosy, I do prefer big, wet, soft and floaty women! Perhaps some of them prefer small, thin, tight and twisted men? I do hope so.

I do like going out to places, and it's not always what I do when I get there that is the thing I like. I actually like just going around in the big blue minibus that always seems to be there for us, ready when we are and want to go somewhere. I'm sure I'll have told you this before, but I really like it when we are moving about going somewhere, with all the low-down humming and the jiggling of my chair, and the whooshing sounds and lights and sights that fly past the windows. Yes, it's much better than that '*Pointless*' thing, even I don't do much when I get there, wherever there is. Yes, I like the moving and jiggling sensations as we go along, they can make me feel more alive, as if I am doing more myself, being more active, moving more, living more, having more of a life. Even if I'm actually just sat in my chair in the back of the minibus.

So, when I'm in the minibus, I find there is already a sense of expectation in there, as if its waiting for me. And I feel that expectation. When we're moving in the minibus, I feel some sense of purpose, that we're going somewhere to do something for some reason, even if I don't know what it actually is. So, I feel that purpose. In the minibus there also seems to be a sense or togetherness with the others in there with me. And I feel that, I get what that is about. We are going somewhere together. It isn't just me, and there will be a purpose to it, a purpose to the journey, something is going to happen when we get there.

I don't know what it will be, what we'll do or see when we get there, but it might be something nice and something familiar, it often is. It might not be, though. So, I get those feelings, expectation, purpose and togetherness. I get all those feelings as we move along with the lights and sights flashing past the windows. This is living, yes, surely it is. And the travelling, the getting there, often feels better than the thing that happens when we arrive. But that doesn't matter, it's travelling, it's moving, it's living, it broadens the mind; it adds a sense of something a bit extra.

This sense of expectation is a funny thing though. I kind of sense it even though I can't properly look forward into the future. Not like I guess you can, predicting, even at time fully knowing what is coming, what is going to happen soon, what is going to happen tomorrow, what is going to happen the day after, and next week, next month, next year. I can't project my mind forward like that, not in the way that you probably can, not forward into a future time that is yet to come. For me it is all just really what is happening now, in the present. Although I suppose I do know some of the sequences of things, of very familiar things. In that way I can perhaps sense what's supposed to come next, but not very clearly, not like you.

Although I do have a sense of the past, not proper, clear recollections of things I have seen and done in the past; not clear memory pictures that I can recall from somewhere. No mental 'in-my-head' images of things from the past to be retrieved from somewhere and brought back into my mind at will. No, that's not possible for me. But I do have a sense of things past, like a personal mental familiarity with familiar things, but only with really familiar activities and sensations and experiences. I suppose you'll be wanting an example. Okay, so I do know things about familiar people, I do know their voices and their movements, but I can't use all that kind of memory and familiarity stuff to think about the future, to project my mind forward and imagine what they will be doing tomorrow. No that is too much for me.

Although, to be honest, it doesn't really bother me. How could it? I don't know that I can't do it, so I don't struggle trying to do it. Remember, this is how I am, and this is how I have always been. I don't know any other way of being. So, I don't really know that there is a future out there before me, various possible futures that I might need to consider, to think about. It just never occurs to me that there is going to be one of all possible futures out there ahead of when and where I am now. I don't have the idea of it, I've never developed that concept. So, I don't fret about it. I don't give it a second thought, actually I don't even give it a first …

I do know some things …

You know, actually I do know some things. It might not be quite the same as you, and certainly nowhere near as much, but I do have some knowledge about the world, I do know some things that you would call facts. For starters, I know that I am human, I think that it is a fact that I know that I am one of you, that you are one of me, that we are all one of us. Yes, I might not know a lot of things, and that's certainly true, but I do know that I am not a thing, that I am not like the things that are here around me. I know that there is more to me than that. I know that I am here, here where I am just now, now back out of the sensory room and back in the room with my bed in it. And I know that I am one of the people who live here. I know that I am one person among other people. I know that we are kind of the same because somehow we relate to each other, that we get on better than we do with the other non-people things around us. I suppose I know this because we are more the same than the other things around me which are more different than we are.

Yes, that's a fact that I know. I don't actually know how I know it, but I know it just the same. I suppose I know that because somehow we can naturally connect with each other, somehow act together doing the same thing at the same time. Yes, and I know that we are naturally drawn to each other in some way, for some reason. I don't really know why it is, this intense interest in each other, and what we all do, but it is certainly there, as a fact. Perhaps it is because there aren't many of us, not so many of us compared to the other things, those other thingy kinds of things that are all around us. Perhaps that's why we feel drawn to each other. Perhaps that's why we club together, to feel safer in the world of other things, to feel a sense of togetherness, to feel that we are not alone. Perhaps.

One of the things that sets us, me and you, apart from the other things is the way we move, the way we act, the whole person as a person thing. People move differently to things, do different things, have some essential quality that we all share, and I know that. Although having said all that, we are all different as well, us people. That's the interesting thing about us, we are the same and yet we are all different. And I can tell that as well. Even though we are all the same, and we move differently from things, at the same time we move a bit differently from each other. We do different things than things, and also different things from each other. But I still know the difference.

Yes, people do sometimes act more or less the same but differently. They often move more or less the same but somehow a bit differently from each other, and it's hard to say just how that is; even with the people I know very well. Trying to pin-point these differences is really tricky.

But for me the thing that is special about how someone moves is that it is often the first thing that I can recognise people by, so there is difference in there somewhere. It's not so much the shape of their bodies that differs, although they do and I can sense that as well, the height of their faces and things like that, where their eyes are, and where their smiles come out from, but it's how their bodies move about in just slightly different ways, each with slightly different body movements and rhythms. That's the thing that marks them out for me.

Yes, it's that their bodies make different shapes in time, different people having different rhythms, like there is a different pulse to how some people move. Yes, mixed in with the big obvious movements there are other smaller movements as well, little flourishes and shapes that give them away as to who they are, and also to what they are about. Small additions or differences in the way they hold bits of themselves, in the shape they make with their bodies. A slight lift here or a small quick dip there, a steady bobbing of the top part, a different angle in the way they are standing, stuff like that. A slow pause before a quick dart of the hand, only slight, but there all the same; it's often how I tell people apart, especially if they aren't that close, or if they are quiet.

It's how they move and how they hold themselves that gives them away to me, and I can sometimes tell what they are about to do by the way they move. Especially if it isn't going to be pleasant, I will get a few moments warning by sensing something different in the way they come towards me.

Anyway, I'm awake now and have been put back in my room with the bed. My bedroom I suppose you'd call it. They must have put me here when I fell asleep in the sensory room. And now I sense that they will be coming to get me soon. It's easy that one, I can smell it, the time that is. I can smell that something is afoot, and I'll be out of here soon back into the feeding room. But not yet. I suppose I'm in here for a bit of a change, literally a change of some of my under stuff. I won't go into any details, that wouldn't be nice for either of us. But I'll be clean and dry again down there in no time. Enough said!

But they will be back soon, the staff, to come and get me, and that will be nice as well. I can hear the others getting noisy out there, my other people, the ones I live with. They must know that something is about to happen, Margaret, Ian, Brian and Eddie. I can hear their noises; well, I can clearly hear Margaret. She's not shrieking like she was last night, more burbling now with a more content tone to her sounds. I know all their sounds as I've lived with them for as long as I can remember. In fact, I can't remember ever being without them. They have always been around me, them, and there were others as well, but certainly always them.

Actually, while I've got a few moments …

Actually, while I've got a few moments, perhaps a quick bit of personal history wouldn't go amiss, for us both I suppose. Yes, perhaps a bit about how it was when I was young, a bit of history about the place I grew up. The 'hospital' it was called, by polite people, on the kids' 'ward', me and all the others, including Margaret, Ian and Brian.

Once again, being honest, as that is in my character (both real, and as imagined here), I can't actually remember. No, not to bring it back into my mind as an image, an image centred around me. No, and perhaps fortunately for me, I can't remember the rows of metal beds, with high cot sides, in the big open, starkly lit rooms. No, I can't really remember the rows of beds with the small and twisted bodies of their occupants, someone's unwanted, abandoned or unmanageable offspring; we as children.

Yes, fortunately I can't really remember the damp grey walls and dark brown curtains, or the cockroaches that scuttled away under the beds at night. They were certainly there, but I can't actually remember them. No, I really can't, and a good job really. And the smell, it's a good job that I can't remember that awful blend of bodily waste and floral disinfectant. No, that's gone, or locked away so far down that I won't ever be able to fetch it back. Yes, good job really.

You see, there are some hidden advantages to having such a profound intellectual disability; and not remembering sometimes being one of them. Although I suppose it would be nice to remember some of those men and women, mainly women, who looked after us then. Actually, hospital nurses they were, with all the uniforms and that, nice and familiar and, well I suppose, uniform; not like now. I couldn't say how well qualified these nurses were, at nursing, but they all looked smart, and that was a big thing back then. Yes, I would like to remember some of them, the soft and enveloping motherly ones, the cuddly ones that really cared, and that was most of them. But it wasn't all of them, no not all. I'm glad I can't remember those other ones.

Anyway, that was then, and this is now. And I am now still living with some of the same people that I grew up with, the same ones who went into the hospital as kids, and the same ones who were then moved out as middle-aged adults into homes like the one we have now, this place here. We didn't ask to move, none of us could, but moved we were. One day there, in a hospital, the next here, in a home, neither being a choice we made. It was all decided for us.

But really it is okay, here that is. Actually, it is much, much better; warmer, friendlier, cleaner smelling, more stimulating, and with less scuttling, scurrying under-bed wildlife (luckily, there's actually none of them scuttlers here now!). Actually, they aren't all the same. Mark isn't with us anymore, he had to be taken out with a sheet over his face, and then he was replaced in his room by Eddie, a much quieter chap. Quiet in his own way, although he does a lot of breathing, heavy breathing, I mean seriously heavy breathing, loudly puffing and huffing away like a good 'un. He's the best breather we have in the house. Perhaps that's why they brought him in, being a good breather after Mark stopped with his. I'm sure he could win prizes for his breathing, if they gave them out for that kind of thing, always breathing, that's Eddie for you … shame Mark couldn't do the same!

Anyway, always being always together means that Margaret, Ian, and Brian, and increasingly Eddie with his breathing, well, they are familiar, they have always been there, and here, and I like that. I must have said it loads of time, but remember my memory is rubbish, but I like what I know, and I only get to know something if it is really familiar.

I've already told you about Margaret and her screeching and hitting, and that does grate with me, but I suppose I would miss it if she wasn't here, the screeching that is. And Ian, well Ian is probably the most cheerful man who has ever not walked the earth, what with being in a chair like me. But he is really, really, really cheerful; he laughs out loud at just about anything and everything. I don't know why he finds it all so funny, and I don't suppose he knows either, but he certainly does, and his happy sounds can at times be infectious. He can sometimes cheer me up when we spend some time together, if we're placed together in the front room. He'll be away laughing to himself, and that brightens me up too. Yes, that's nice is that. Ian, yes, he's a right good un. And then there is Brian.

Brian's a bit different. For a start he's learned to walk, so he doesn't need to be in chair all the time. He can and often does wander about the house when we are at home, but actually he tends to keep himself to himself. He seems to be a bit of a loner, stays a bit separate. He ups and offs if the rest of us are in the front room together. No, he's not keen on a crowd isn't our Brian, and for him it's as if two's a crowd. He's okay, don't get me wrong, we rub along fine together, always have, but he's always moving away when I see him. To be honest, I'm not sure if I ever really seen his face!

And probably, if I could walk, I might be a bit like him, if I could choose to. Not all the time, because I like having people around. But just imagine having the freedom to wander off, to find your own quiet space, just when you wanted to, a place to choose to be in just by yourself. Imaging that. But I can't, so there it is.

No, I'm in my chair almost all the time I'm out of my bed. And I don't have the hands or the arms or the coordination or the strength to move it, even if I wanted to. Actually, after all these years, not ever remembering otherwise, I now feel that my chair is really part of me, when I'm in it that is. Until then, until I'm in it, then actually it's just a thing, just a piece of characterless furniture, empty and unmoving. But when I'm in it, well then it becomes part of me, an integral part of the person. The chair instantly becomes an outer extension of the person I am, framing me, shaping me, carrying me. It both holds me still and makes me mobile, at once holding me captive and freeing me to be upright and be moved about. Yes, it somehow supports me to be in the world and separates me from it.

Okay, okay, let's not get too deep here; it's a chair. Yes, to you it's probably just a chair, but to me it is my chair, Harry's chair, and I couldn't really be Harry without it.

Oh, it's moving again. I've had the tap, the whisper in the ear, and now the moving forwards. Here I go, in the chair, in my chair, through to the feeding room. I thought it might be anytime soon ... and then, wham bam, within a couple of minutes, it'll all be done. I'll be full again.

Did you ever wonder what it might be like ...

Maybe now's a good time, sat here in the feeding room waiting to be injected with my tea, to ask you something? All this stuff here about me, and now that we are getting on so well, yes, maybe it's time to ask something of you? So, this is the question I would put to you:

Did you ever wonder, even for a moment, what it might be like to have no words? To have to live and to think without any words to help you? ... and even if you ever did, which I guess you probably won't have done, I bet you used words to think about it, to help you do your thinking then. How could you otherwise?

But I don't have that luxury. I have to do all my thinking differently, in my own way. Yes, I have to think as best I can, use what I've got to think with, and that doesn't include any kind of real, symbolic, clearly representative words. So, I can't think like you do, I can't build up my thoughts bit by bit, with words put into a particular order to represent what I think.

I have to have thoughts directly taken from the things I am doing, in that moment, and all at once, as an entire thought or feeling or sensation. So, at times, times like now, sat here in the feeding room waiting to be tube fed, I have a kind of visual thinking process, a present-tense consciousness coming straight out of my senses.

But there is more to it than that. I also have an accompanying awareness of my associated feelings mixed in with the conscious senses stuff. Sometimes that feels very clear to me, but if there's a bit too much going on, then it can become too much for me to process, and it all goes hazy and indistinct. If there is way too much stuff going on, well then it all breaks up into a dizzying swirl of mixed-up sensations and feelings, and then I can't make any sense of it all. At those times I just shut down, shut it all out, pull myself inside myself and away from everything else.

But, in the real world that you encounter, outside of this book, I couldn't describe any of it; because that would take words, and that is where I get stuck. So, I can't separate my thoughts out by themselves and translate them into your kind of language; not in the way that you think you can. I can't detach my thinking from me being in the here and now, and from what's currently coming into me through my senses. So, for me, what's going on in my head is always much more direct and immediately connected with what I'm currently experiencing in the real world around me. Although I guess that can be the same for you sometimes, actually maybe quite often, but it's always the case for me.

I shouldn't try to make my thinking stuff sound too simple. No, I'm not simple, and my thoughts aren't simple either. I do recognise familiar things, and familiar experiences, but I do it without attaching names and labels to them. Instead, it's all about the relationship something has directly with me, so I tend to recognise things for what they might do for me, or even do to me … so it isn't about what they are themselves as recognisable and separate things. No, it isn't about what things are called or what they look like, or where they've come from. My thinking is more generally sensing and feeling what some thing can or will do to or for me, whether that is nice thing or a not so nice thing.

So yes, it's all about what relationship something has with me. So, when I see or feel something, some sensation, some perception, what my mind does is really quickly try to tell me what something will do …

Will it feed me or make me feel fed?

Will it make me feel less thirsty?

Will it make me cold? Or warm? Or hot?

Will it hurt me?

Will it disturb me?

Will it make me comfortable?

Will it go inside me or through a bit of me?

Will it entertain me or stimulate my body somehow?

Will it tickle?

So, I don't see the things as what they are, and then decide what they might do to me, I just tend to sense the 'what will this thing do to me' bit straight away. And really, isn't that the most important thing, whether the thing will be good or bad at doing good or bad things to me. I think that's the most important thing, what essential use is it, this thing, and might it be kind or might it be cruel. That's more important to me than what label or word it's known by. Things are what they are to me, what they can or will give me, not what label I, or you, might give them. I think that thinking is easier that way; and more effective. Well, it is for me, it's all I can do. I use what I've got, I have to, I have no other way.

As I still sit here, looking around at what I can make out, trying to focus in on things out of the sides of my eyes, all those things out there, I'm looking for the things that might do things to me and for me. I'm looking out for the familiar things that make up my familiar world. However, I don't know their names. I don't know what they're called. Perhaps some aren't called anything. Perhaps there are some things, perhaps lots of things, that don't have names or words attached to them, not just by me, but by anyone. I don't know, perhaps.

Yes, perhaps there are loads of things out there that have never had a name, that people don't think about, or can't think about because they don't have the words to label them as a particular something. Where would that leave us all (well you actually)? Yes, loads and loads of things staying out of everyone's minds because no one has as yet given them a word. Well, you'd be just like me really, in blissful ignorance, utterly unknowing, not even knowing that you don't know something, because you couldn't think about the absence of something you didn't know about; all for the sake of not having a word. Perhaps that's so, perhaps we are more alike than you think?

Just think about it, this language thing; remember, you'll have to because I can't. But this language thing has me puzzled. So, what happens if you want to describe an entirely new thing, where do you start? Would you start with the thing, the thing itself without, as yet, any words to describe it, and see if you could conjure up something at the time, once you realised it was a something without a name? Or perhaps you could start by trying to make up some spare words, words you haven't used yet to label the things you still don't know about, and use one of them when the need arises? Sort of attach a word as you go along. Although won't you have to agree this with everyone else who also uses the same words and language? It all seems way too complicated for my liking.

But actually, my experiences might be useful here, because this is mostly what my life and being me is like. You see I have loads of things in my life, just about all of them, that I don't have labels to name them with, or words explain them with. Perhaps, just perhaps, that's been a benefit to me? Perhaps because I don't use words to label and describe things for myself, perhaps I'm not limited by them, perhaps there are things I see and feel and experience that you don't because you don't have the right words? You never know, there might be, and you wouldn't, couldn't know about them, because of the way you think with your limited list of words. Perhaps that holds you back?

It would be interesting to exchange our thoughts and feelings on this, but where would we start? How could we share our thoughts and feelings with no shared language or experience, no common ground to build an understanding on? Again, I'm afraid I can't help, I really don't know … do you?

If we ever could share our thoughts and feelings with each other, directly that is, for you to get to know about my visual and sensory in-the-moment understanding of what is going on, to try to give you an insider view of being me, being in my head, well to be honest it wouldn't help that much. Because in reality, without you being me, living all my life as I have, it wouldn't make any sense to you. You wouldn't understand any of it because you couldn't understand how I understand things.

But once again, perhaps we are more alike than you think. How much of what you see and feel, and experience, can you put directly into words? How much can you really fully describe? Every bit of it entirely? How it feels, completely? What it all means to you, absolutely?

Not much of it I reckon. I bet you can't really and fully and exactly describe all the things that happen to you, and how you feel about it all, even to yourself, never mind to anyone else. No, I reckon we aren't that different really, not with the sensing and feeling and thinking and labelling and stuff like that. For both of us, I reckon most of it stays unsaid and un-described. For both of us, most of it stays unnamed and unlabelled. For all of us most of it stays un-worded, just stuff that's there happening or present in the world around us, being without being thought about or said, all for the sake of some missing words. Who'd have thought it? Certainly not me.

Oh, here we go, the lady is leaning over me, she's doing the feeding, the making me full thing. But actually, there's more to this operation than just that. There's also that language thing going on again, that talking and words and stuff. Yes, some sounds and noises coming from her, "blather, blather, blather", and I can't understand a single word of it, not a word. But I am grateful for it. The words themselves might be meaningless, to me that is, but it certainly isn't pointless; far from it. For me the sense of it isn't in the words, not in the symbolic bits that seem to go together to make it all up. No, the meaning exists somewhere else, woven somewhere in amongst the overall doing, her overall being. Somewhere in the sounds I associate a friendliness, an act of being a social. That's where the message lies, somewhere in the tone and the tempo and the flow, somewhere packaged in amongst all the other stuff, the looks she gives me, the nods of her head, the smiles, the small and special nudges from her elbows, all that taken together is the message; that's what she's saying to me.

And anyway, together all of it is much more than the words could ever manage to say themselves. When it's all put together into some action, then it becomes meaningful. It says that she wants to do it, do it for me, that she seems to enjoy it, that she seems to enjoy being with me. Yes, she says that she likes hanging out with me, that she appreciates my company. She's telling me that, and probably only that, but that is more than enough.

It's certainly enough for me. I think we both get that, the social bit, the connection bit, the being together, enjoying each other … and I like it. Actually, I really like her! I bet you would too.

'Beneath the noise, below the din
I hear a voice, it's whispering
In science and in medicine
I was a stranger
You took me in'

(U2: Miracle Drug)

I've been put back in my room now …

I've been put back in my room now, for a bit of quiet time. Presumably to chill for a bit after tea, before all the bedtime stuff starts; the bathing and cleaning routine, with the staff themselves having a bit of a break before getting us ready for our night-time sleep. So, I'm technically on my own. But often, as now for example, I can hear voices around the place. People aren't talking to me, and as I've said so many times now, I wouldn't be able to tell you anything of what they are saying, but I do still get a comfort from hearing the human voice.

It's nice to be surrounded by the gentle hubbub (is that a word?) of fellow human beings getting on with their stuff, being around, filling the space and time around me with the sounds of being busy and social and alive. And if I can somehow feel somehow included by the people doing it, the busy doing stuff talking, then I like it.

However, there are times, if I haven't had much attention for a while, and when the people and their voices seem a bit far away, then it can also then make me feel a bit out of it, a bit away and isolated, even a bit lonely. You see, if I haven't had much social stuff for a while, I can then start to feel somehow separated from those voices, aware that I am apart from them and their social stuff. Then, to me they can seem like disembodied voices without faces, ghostly human sounds coming in from behind the walls, and as I am unable to move towards them, unable to actively become part of their social goings-on, then it feels a bit like I'm not really there, or not there enough. Then I can start to feel like I am too insignificant to be a proper part of their mutual togetherness. Then I can get a bit sad about it … I reckon you would too, if you were in my shoes; well, actually stuck here in my chair.

And while I'm on the subject of talking around me, and not to me, sometimes it can actually irritate me if I feel that the talking is all around me, but I'm deliberately not part of it. Or when I sense that the talking is about me, with people using my name, but it isn't to me. When the talking is around me, when its faceless voices talking above me, at the side, behind my back, not to me or with me. I can sense that, sense the separation. Then I feel the distance, some kind of invisible barrier, a sense of social exclusion.

I know the talk is not for me this time, and that is okay at the moment. And anyway, I am powerless to change it, even if I wanted to. I feel powerless a lot of the time; I kind of know my own limitations, after all I have had a lifetime to learn this kind of stuff. I generally know when I can do something, which isn't often, and I suppose therefore I also know when I can't, which is much of the time. I know when it's worth a try to do something, and when it's not; I kind of know that through experience. Indeed, I often know that with some people that it's not worth actually trying with them, to communicate with them, they are too involved in their lives and their own actions. So, I don't even bother; not with them.

That's the best teacher, experience, you can't argue with it or disbelieve it. Experience is what it is, no more and no less. Things happen, so I just get used to it and learn to go along with the facts of life, the simple facts of experience. That's what I do, I go along with stuff that happens day in day out. I am myself; I do what I can, and I forget the rest. Although the forgetting stuff is something that I am really pretty good at, and so that comes quite naturally for me.

Perhaps we are sponges of experience. Perhaps that's what happens. We just soak life up like a sponge in the bath, holding onto to some of it, letting other stuff dribble away unnoticed. Yes, we accumulate experiences both wanted and unwanted. Relentlessly it comes, a lot of it uninvited, actually almost all of it uninvited by me, the good, the bad and the in-between, stacking up to make a life. My life, and your life; that's all getting a bit deep now, isn't it. But it means that in that sense we are just the same, at least partial products of our life's experiences.

Although actually, I'm generally only a recipient of my own experiences. You see, most of my experiences are organised and directed by other people, and I'm just there having them. That's because generally I am unable to take a lead, I am unable to switch experiences on and off as I might choose. So often I become an object of other's choices, doing or having other people's preferred experiences, sat here with most of it washing over me. But I suppose some of it I do absorb, and so some of it is useful to me. But a lot of it, actually most of it flows by me unnoticed, going past me and on to somewhere or someone else, rippling out to other people to become their experiences rather than mine. That really is where I lack the power to change things, to lead on things, to do more things myself as and when I want.

However, let's not knock this experience thing altogether. I have found through experience that some things seem to have much more about them than other things, more presence, more impact as part of their make-up, as part of their being. Through experience alone I know that some things make a bigger mark on me and my world than some other things, even things much bigger than they are. Some things push in on my world, sometimes more than they really deserve, like a little crease in the cloth of my trousers, or a tiny bit of dust in the eye, a bit of phlegm stuck in the throat, a small word said sharply. Small things, yes, but they can cause all sorts of long-lasting difficulties.

The nice, easy going along character of my world can sometimes be shattered by the smallest thing, my peace and composure blown away by a sometimes barely perceptible entity, like a bit of well matured phlegm. And yet really big things, things like the ceiling or the sky don't seem to do anything. Massive things that barely make a mark, leave no sign of their presence. They just sort of stay there, big and full but barely noticeable in my great scheme of things. It's their lack of any direct consequence to me I suppose. Things so big and yet not worth a second glance. But a bit of phlegm at the back of the throat, out of coughing range, or a small but coarse crumb stuck under a buttock, agony! Who'd have thought it?

I also find it's the same with people. Some people seem to have a load of that power of presence stuff, as a part of their make-up. They somehow make a bigger mark. But also, in some ways other people just don't, make muck of a mark that is. Some people can't be around without them having a strong effect on me, one way or the other, and yet others I hardly notice at all. And you can't often say why or what it is, this presence thong. Some people just have more of it (whatever it is) than others. Although I also think sometimes less is, or can be more, if their kind of presence isn't the kind you want, nor when you want it, if you know what I mean. Although at other times more is more if that person has just the right kind of it, the good kind of presence. And I find that out with experience. There's no hard and fast rule to this presence thing. I can't predict it, although actually I can't predict hardly anything.

Generally, though, it seems to be people that have the most presence, most of the time. They affect me, and maybe you as well, the most. In fact, they seem to affect everything about the place much more than they deserve to. Yes, people cast a big shadow with this presence thing they have. When they are around me, say here in the room with me, my attention is always are drawn towards them. Generally, no matter what else is there around me, it is the people in that space that seem to fill it most. Maybe you feel the same about it. And then we can't help ourselves from somehow focusing in on them, on their presence, somehow feeding off their actions and emotions as they share that space and time with us.

This invisible presence that draws us in, that some people have, seems to be beyond our control. It is just there, coming out from them and then getting into the heads of others. That's what I find. Somehow, we seem to automatically share our human feelings with those others around us, whether we like it or not. If it was you in the room with me (let's just pretend, shall we), if it was you then you would somehow affect me and my mood, and my feelings and thoughts, just by being with me. But also, I reckon I would do the same to you, so my emotions and my feelings would affect you. Yes, you would certainly think and feel differently in my presence than you would if I wasn't there. And hopefully the same back.

Yes, my experience is that, whether we like it or not, as people we are somehow invisibly tied together, our thoughts and feelings projecting out there, getting into each other's heads, sneaking out and sneaking into the minds of others. It's a bit scary to think like that, the effects it can have, our minds somehow belonging a bit to one another, not just to ourselves. Oh dear, yes, a bit scary!

When you think about it, actually we as people are all in some way entangled with each other, dependant on each other for so much. All of us, no matter who we are, we are dependent on others for somethings. Yes, for something to do, for someone to be with, for someone to be friends with, for someone to love. We need others to live around, to live with, to make our lives what they are. We need other people to do stuff with us, other people to do stuff for us, other people to give us things, other people to take things away for us, other people to help us think and feel and be ourselves. Perhaps that's something we all share, me, you, everyone. Yes, I think probably that's true.

Overall, you know, I don't really expect too much out of life. So, I'm generally not disappointed by it, by my life and my experiences. There are certainly things and experiences that I like to happen, and things and experiences that I don't like. But I don't spend any time worrying about things or feeling let down by people if things don't always go my way. You see I am someone who has got used to having experiences come my way. I don't, no, I can't go out of my way to get stuff for myself or create my own experiences. So, it's best to be this way, not worrying about things, not being disappointed, not expecting things to be better, or different, or anything really.

So, I just tend to live in the here and the now, accepting what comes my way. I will just sit or lay here, having the experience of what and who is around me, and mostly liking it, mostly enjoying what and who is around me. Living for and in the moment, living my kind of life and sharing it with lots of other people, people I like (mostly) and people who help and care for me (mostly). That's not bad that, not really, not most of the time.

Oh, it looks like I'm off again. I'm suddenly on the move, being pushed out of my room, quiet time over, something is on the agenda. I can tell by the speed of my being pushed, someone has some task in mind, and I'm going to get it whatever it is. It's bath time again. Great; getting wet, getting warm, getting splashed, getting rubbed, getting dried, getting dressed. Great; clean and warm night clothes on, and then back out to the telly room for a bit as the carers bath the others.

There's a bit of a draft here, where I am …

There's a bit of a draft here now, where I am, here in my chair and in my loose night clothes. These drafts, they often seem to seek me out, find out where I am and then really focus in on me. More than that, they seem to focus on particular bits of me, and I can't do anything about it. Yes, these crafty drafty bits of coldness sneak in along my body, starting with the outside smaller places, especially at the ends, and then work their way up and in. Usually at my feet and legs first, and then sometimes in and at my hands, stealing the heat bit by bit and replacing it with a chilly numbness. Robbing my outside extremities of their warmth and feeling, silently extracting all the heat. You can't see or hear it happening, well I can't, and I guess nor can the staff, but in they come these sneaky, unseen drafts.

After a while, the chill can really take hold. With my circulation I'm defenceless against even the smallest and weakest of drafts. Up and in they creep, up along my legs and arms, in around the neck and ears, sucking all their post-bath warmthness out. Instead, in comes its coldness; light and kind of tickly at first, then heavier and more intense, numbing the flesh, tightening its grip, pressing in, taking all my attention with it. And I can't tell anyone. There are times when I can't think about anything else but the incoming chill carried in on its sly and sneaky draft.

If it's there for long enough, the draft, then it robs me both of my warmth and attention. If it's there for long enough then my attention takes itself off into the cold areas of my body, so everything else loses focus. I have to shut my eyes when the drafts are really bad. I can't look out when the cold is getting all the way in, as my attention chooses to focus inwards. I can't just ignore it; I have to feel it. It draws me fully into the cold places, at the edges, all my senses coming together to feel the sharp edge of the cold front moving up my legs and arms. But no one else know this, knows that the drafts have found me again as I can't ever tell them. If only I could speak, then I could tell them. But I can't, and I can't ever hope to. That's just the way it is, and perhaps that's why the drafts find me, perhaps they know I can't tell anyone about them. So, I just remain silent, wordlessly at its's mercy, powerless to dodge the draft.

I know I've been on about this before, but just because I can't speak, just because I'm wordless, it doesn't mean I don't have feelings. And I'm having them now, both physical and emotional. Emotional feelings, thoughts of sorts. You can call them what you like, feelings, emotions, senses, moods, thoughts, opinions, likes, dislikes. Yes, label them as you like, they make up my experience of the world. Or at least my personal experience of my experiences of the world. So, what's the real difference. It's my inner reaction to my outer experiences. It's how I come to know about all about the stuff I know about, have a view on, have reactions to. Not the wordy thoughts like you might have, but the stuff underneath, the stuff from where your wordy thoughts come from.

Those underneath the surface thoughts that you might feel but not express, I have plenty of those. And they are real to me as they would be to you, like when I'm cold. It's just I can't translate them into words, into a voice in my head, or a voice out of my mouth to do anything about them. But I feel them swirling around in me, not really inside my head, but like now, with the drafty coldness, feelings emerging from my body. It washes in and up me, making things happen inside, making me feel things, making me do things, making me look at things or shut my eyes not to. These feelings popping up inside me in response to stuff coming in from the outside, stuff like cold, or hot, stuff like quiet or loud, stuff like being still or moving about, or feeling wet or feeling dry, stuff like feeling comfortable or not feeling comfortable, knowing when things are too tight or too loose, knowing when I'm feeling tired or when I'm feeling really happy. I know all these feelings, in and out they come and go, sensations and feelings, and yes, kinds of thoughts really, about what I like, what I don't like, what I want to keep going, what I want to stop happening, like the crafty drafty coldness sneaking in, stuff like that. I have that stuff in my body and in my head, making all of it meaningful to me; but not to others, as I can't tell them about it.

Thank goodness, here comes some help. And again, with a tap, and a pat, and a quiet whisper in my ear, I'm off into my room now. Off to my room for a bit of a quiet time. Yes, and there, she's parked me up, brakes on. Then down go the lights. Not off, but dimmer, and there's some nice relaxing music now wafting my way.

I can feel the day winding down from here on in, and I'm really quite ready for it. It's my familiar evening time routine, so I can relax and let it all happen. I can also now feel the feeling edging back into my feet, into hands, arms and legs; luckily the draft hasn't followed me in here.

I can sit back in my chair and relax and feel the warmth return. Yes, that's a nice feeling, I like that, and I can have a bit of time exploring my belt strap buckle, there at my shoulder, my trusty companions. I haven't checked it for a while, what with the cold taking my attention elsewhere, so I can just move my chin across to check on it now, just to see that it's still okay and still the same. Yes, it is, just there, just where it should be, just there again. Yes, it hasn't moved. No, it isn't any different. Just there, same as before, just where it normally is, right at the right point as I rub my chin over it, just the same … well that's a relief.

The songs are in your eyes
I see them when you smile
I've had enough of romantic love
I'd give it up, yeah, I'd give it up
For a Miracle Drug, for a Miracle Drug
Miracle, Miracle Drug'

(U2: Miracle Drug)

It's properly getting dark now …

It's properly getting dark now. Things are slowing down and quietening down. I can hear others being moved to their rooms as well. It will soon feel right to call time on the day, and then be put into bed. I know this bit, the familiar routine of being hoisted into bed and gently wedged into place. This is what normally comes next, after the dimming of the lights and the playing of the quiet music. Anyway, I am starting to feel a bit sleepy now. I'm a bit 'in and out' of being awake, half there and half not quiet.

As I've said before, I don't get much in the way of really good deep sleep. During the day I have a lot of naps, my day punctuated by short periods of drifting off and drifting back, eyes stuttering between open and shut. My tired eyes crossing and uncrossing as I try and fail to focus on something tangible and stimulating; like now, with my increasingly sleepy eyes aimlessly wandering the featureless grey above me.

And so, I wait for what is coming, the being put to bed routine. I have a sense of it coming, it being a regular feature of my daily pattern of life. I can feel it edging towards me on its usual, recurring wave of time. After my bath, in my room, warm and relaxed, with this quiet and soothing music. I know it's coming soon. I've heard it many, many times before, the easy rhythm, quiet and slow, cushioning me ready for what's next. Gently getting in my head, letting me know what's expected of me, helping get there and get it done.

It's my turn now. Someone's coming to put me to bed. I can hear her voice as she comes in the room, warm and soothing.

I can smell her smell; a certain musty smell when she gets up close, sorting out the straps to hoist me up and over. It all seems to fit together really well: the warmth, the music, the shadows, the voice, the smell, my slackening breaths, my wandering eyes, my already half-dozing ... and now up and into my bed; cushions and wedges now in place.

Have you ever listened to your own breathing, though? Really listened? Have you actually listened to the sound it makes when you move the air in and out of your body? I do when there isn't much of anything else going on. Sometimes I focus in and listen really intently, sometimes for ages.

That's what I'm doing now that I am in bed, now that the music has stopped, and the lights have been turned down to the point that I can't make anything out. This is when I start to listen to my breathing. Yes, listening to myself actually living, the air going in and down and around and up and out again; before it all starts again. And when you really listen you can actually sense some moments when you stop to take a bit of a rest from it, when you stop to take a breather from your breathing; well, I do. Interestingly, well to me interestingly, the harder you listen the longer the rest bits seem to get, and then you have to wait. You then wait for it all to start again, waiting with bated breath, will it come again? And which turn is it? Is it in or is it out first this time? Who knows. But then it does start again.

It's as if the breathing knows itself what it needs to do and when it needs to do it; when it's supposed to be in, when it's supposed to be out. It's a good job it does really because I can never remember myself. If it was up to me, I'd probably get it all wrong. I'd be trying to breath in when it should be out, and out when it should be in. And with all the too intently listening and the waiting, I might drift off and forget to start again. That wouldn't be any good, not for anyone, waiting and forgetting all about the breathing, my attention taken by something else outside of me, and the breathing still holding back and waiting, waiting for some kind of signal, an invitation to start again, something to let it know that the waiting was over, and the breathing should start again.

No, it's a good job the breathing knows what to do for itself and doesn't need my help. But it is interesting to listen to, really listen that is, trying to work out the pattern of it. And when you listen you realise just how noisy it all is, really loud really. And just how relentlessly tiring it all is; it's exhausting at times. Yes, just on their own, the breathing and the listening, neither of which normally takes much out of you, but together they can completely drain you. So, at times like now, at this time of the day, I'm just here, just listening in the quiet of the house to my own noises, luckily for now my breathing just getting on, doing its own thing. I can feel my own living rhythm, nice and steady, and it is familiar and reassuring. It helps me feel even more tired, and so it all slows itself, easing off in anticipation of what's ahead, slowly slowing, steadily winding itself down.

Remember then: in then out, out then in. And then again, just keeping it going, in the right order. And promise me you won't stop when I'm not awake enough to check on you …

Actually, in all the time I've been alive …

Actually, in all the time I've been alive I have never given a single thought as to why the people who care for me, care for me. Yes, why these people, my staff, come around here every day to do all this stuff for me, to me or with me. I suppose it might be an interesting thing to muse on for a while, if I could (and yes, I do realise I can't - well actually I don't realise I can't, I just can't. But let's not get stuck on that point. Just imagine me musing, if you will? And perhaps you could join in with the musing if you feel comfortable enough).

Well, if I were to muse a while on why these people around me, the ones that come in every day and do the hands-on caring stuff, why they start to come, and why they then keep on coming back, day in day out, well that might be interesting. Although in fact not all of them do keep coming back. Some of them, quite a few actually, only come for a couple of days and then they never return. Yes, very briefly they pop up into my life, do some really private stuff with me, bath me, change me, wipe bits of me clean, and then just as suddenly they stop coming, never to return. But others, well some of them have been coming back for years and years, and years on top of that. So yes, if I could muse, I think I would certainly spend quite some time musing on that.

So, the ones that keep coming back, like the musty smelling lady, why do they do that? What makes some of them return so many times? Often to do just about exactly the same stuff as they did last time they came. And as far as I can tell, most of them seem fairly happy to do so. Not all of them mind, but most of them. Yes, most of them sound pretty happy about it when they chat with me, the tone of their voice seems mainly cheerful, mainly. But who knows why they keep on wanting to do it some more?

Perhaps they get given something nice for doing it? Perhaps they are amply rewarded for their efforts? Or perhaps they do it just because they like doing it? Or like doing it with me? Perhaps they like doing it more than the other things that they might otherwise have to do? So perhaps it is better than any other stuff they might have to do if they weren't here doing the caring stuff? Yes, perhaps they do it to avoid doing other things, other less nice things. Who knows? I don't. I literally can't imagine why they would keep coming back for more.

Maybe it makes them feel good doing these caring types of things here? Maybe also they need to do it for reassurance, knowing its being done properly, the way they think it should be done? Perhaps they do these things simply because for them it's become a kind routine, a routine they can't break out of; just doing it all without thinking?

Perhaps they do it because they feel they have to? Because it is the right thing to do, the correct way to act and be. Perhaps also doing the right thing in the right way is better than doing something else, something wrong. So perhaps doing the pushing around, the bathing, the dressing, the feeding, the changing, the cleaning up, perhaps they are just the right things to do. And once you have done them so often, over so many years, then perhaps it becomes really hard not to do these same things? Perhaps?

Although hopefully, perhaps some of them, the ones that keep on coming back, perhaps they just really like me; okay, us, and like doing things for us. Or maybe its them. Maybe they just want to be liked themselves, liked by us, the people they care for? But who's doing who the biggest favour there then? Whose friendship is the most important, and who are the really needy ones? Hhhmm, that's an interesting question to muse on, if only I could.

Well that really is just about enough for today. My eyes are getting heavy. I'm not too far off with the sleeping now. Although I tend to drift slowly off, I don't do it all at once. I kind of relax into it. I allow the sleep to creep up and gently creep in, a little at a time to start with. So, I'm getting ever more relaxed, warm and comfy, my eyes starting to flicker. I know it won't be long now.

Oh, ehh-up, wait a minute. I was almost there, just slipping into a peaceful state of slumber, but now I'm getting a feeling down below. It's just starting, the sensation of a slow seeping, followed by the leisurely spread of warm dampness. And that's a nice feeling that is, down there in my padded underclothes. That's always a pleasant surprise, nice and warm and damp and comforting. Helping signal the full relaxation of all my muscles at the end of the day. I don't know if that happens for you.

Yes, that feeling of dampness maybe the last sensation we all feel as we drift off. Perhaps it's the last sensation we ever feel? Right at the end of everything, on our final day? No, perhaps as we all drift off to pastures new, perhaps we all have a warm, damp and comforting send off. That can't be a bad way to go, with a slow release, letting it all go, a final warm and damp farewell. That wouldn't be bad to see you on your way, as you float towards the beckoning light of oblivion. No, comforting us all like it was at the start, so it might be at the end; a full circle around, bathed again in warm and wet. That's not a bad way to go I reckon. It's just a thought!

But I'm not on my way out, I might have been close a few times, what with the burning in my chest and all that kind of stuff. But I'm still here, warm, and a bit damp, and definitely alive. Yes, I persist, that's what I do. I suppose that's what I'm good at: persisting. Yes, I can certainly persist at what I'm doing. That's one of the things I'm really good at: laying in bed, sitting in my chair, fiddling with things, listening at sounds, breathing, being alive. Once I get started, I can go on and on at these things. It's one of my strongest points – persistence, often in the face of adversity. But sticking at it, that's me that is, that's what I do. Yes, that's what I'm good at.

No, I'm not on my way out, but wouldn't it be funny if I was. If I passed away right here and now and couldn't finish this thing I'm doing with you. Gone before the proper end. All your effort would have been wasted. But no, I'm fine, just tired and drifting off … asleep that is, not for good.

I wonder what would happen if I did pass on. I've only ever known being alive and being alive as me. So obviously I haven't a clue what would come next. Do you get another go? Is this it, or is it one of a series, like going swimming, getting a bit more used to it and better at it each time? Who know? Do you?

If I did pass on and had another go, would I have to come back as the same sort of person? If not, perhaps I might come back as someone like you, walking and talking and doing all that stuff, perhaps even writing a book like this one. Or perhaps I would have to come back as someone like me, like I am now, there being some kind of predictable uniformity about it. But if I did get another go as someone like you, then perhaps you might come back as some like me, someone who is profoundly disabled? That'd be fair wouldn't it; taking turns, being able to walk or not walk in each other's shoes. Yes, I think that might be a good idea. We'd both then get a better idea what it is like to live as someone else, someone very different. Is that a deal then?

It's strange the things you think of when you're half-asleep, especially if you've just wet yourself ...

'I'd give it up, yeah, I'd give it up
For a Miracle Drug, for a Miracle Drug,
Miracle, Miracle Drug'

(U2: Miracle Drug)

It won't be long now …

It won't be long now, I promise. I'm really nearly fully off this time. I'm slowly easing down through my gears now, and I'll be well off shortly. But I'm just savouring this time, surrendering to the inevitability of sleep. I actually like this time, it's just me and my familiar and cosy surroundings, so long as Margaret doesn't get started again. I feel fully equipped to live this part of my life. I feel that I am perfectly formed to effortlessly be me in this here and now. It's been my life's work really.

But before I go fully off (asleep that is, remember) there's just a couple of things I feel I need to sort out.

Firstly, there's this weird 'U2' stuff that keeps cropping up, that's been included in my book for some strange reason. It wasn't my idea. It sort of sounds great I know, all full of something heartfelt, all sort of nice and positive and all that …

'I'd give it up, yeah, I'd give it up
For a Miracle Drug, for a Miracle Drug,
Miracle, Miracle Drug'

But all this stuff about 'miracles' and 'drugs', what's that all about? Do they think that someone like me is ill and therefore curable or something? Do they think I can be fixed into a better kind of me? That I'm one of them people who is 'locked in' and can understand what is said to them but can't speak or move or whatever?

Now obviously I don't really know what it is they're on about, not really. Are they saying that for someone like me, that my condition is like 'having' something, like a disease or something? But it isn't like that at all. No matter how good the drugs can get, and perhaps the person that wrote it has tried plenty of drugs themselves, but no matter what they give me, I will always be who I am. You can't be cured from being the person you are, and I am Harry, a man with profound and multiple learning disabilities.

No, no miracle drug will cure me from being the person that I have taken a lifetime to become. I was born like this, spent my childhood like this, grew into a man like this, and am happy to remain like this. I am the combined product of who I was born as and all my many lifetime experiences: the good, the bad and the truly awful ones.

Although I bet a lot of people with learning disabilities will have been given plenty of 'miracle' drugs in their time, and probably still are. Although it probably just makes the people who give out the drugs feel better. Perhaps that's why they do it, at least they can feel that they are helping. But do they ever think about what it might be like from our side, the inside side, to have to take this stuff? How differently it makes us think or feel. How it can zone us out, make it even more difficult to think and feel and be ourselves.

But hey-ho, perhaps sometimes the drugs do work, sometimes. Who can really tell; not us. Perhaps they think that if we 'give them a try with this' it's better than using a straitjacket or sticking them in a padded room or giving them electric shocks to the head. And anyway, if it doesn't seem to do anything one way or the other, well, then we can always try them on something else. Who knows? Who cares? Really, who does care? Certainly not me at the moment, I'm way too tired now.

So, one last thing, honest. Before I drift off fully (to hopefully start it all over again tomorrow), I just wanted to have a word about this so-called writing stuff that's been going on here. About this thing with someone writing some kind of 'translation' of my thoughts and feelings here in this book. I just want to make it absolutely clear that I haven't been able to check any of it, not one bit. So, for anything that's been said for me, on my behalf, well I haven't been able to point out any inaccuracies, to correct anything or add any bits that are missing.

No. But given the fact that I am both incapable and powerless in such things, then it will just have to stay as it is, and you will just have to take it 'on trust' that it fairly represents me and my life, just like I have to accept 'on trust' everything that happens to me from those around me. That's just how things are in my life, and in this instance, they are in yours as well. It is as it is, so just suck it up and smile! I smile quite a bit remember.

Anyway, this more or less seems like it then. It feels like an end is coming, and so you will just have to accept this other person's attempt at writing it all out for me – it's probably a load of crap anyway. But it is what it is and make of it what you will. But if any of it is wrong, sounds nonsensical or seems just plain daft, well don't blame me. Remember I didn't write

185

any of it, not a single word – I couldn't, and if I could, I probably I wouldn't want to as nothing really interesting happens to me.

But that doesn't mean I don't have anything interesting to say, or that what I might say wouldn't carry any meaning or significance, or that it wouldn't somehow be worthy or useful to put in front of people. It's just that I couldn't have done this on my own.

Anyway, if you didn't like this book, then it's not my fault, take it up with the guy who wrote it. But if you did like it, then thanks; that's down to me living my life.

So, after this why not look out for me, and people like me. If you see me why not come over and say hello. Don't be shy. But if that can't or doesn't happen, then at the very least perhaps just think of me occasionally, won't you, once in a while. It isn't much to ask, is it?

So how to end this before I drop off into my first bit of deep and restful sleep? If I could divvy up a final deep thought for you to muse on, or perhaps I could end with a clever twist that might lead on to another book (yes, that would be good – Graham), or perhaps it might hint at some miraculous and impending change for the better, perhaps out of nowhere I could suddenly shout out my first clearly articulated …

No, sorry, I'm too tired and I'm going to sleep.

See you around then? Well, possibly.

Ghost writer's epilogue by Graham Firth

Okay Harry, how was that? A fair attempt? A creditable effort would you say, if you could? What would you give me - 3, 4, 5 out of 10? What did you think about the actual writing, did I get you about right? I'm still not even sure that I should actually have done this, all the way through I've felt it's a bit of a con really. And it is isn't it?

All those words are really my words not yours, and you have absolutely no way of answering back if I got any of it wrong. I've completely rewritten it about 5 times now, and still feel I am getting most of it, maybe even all of it, totally and utterly wrong.

But a while ago I did decide to give it go, to try to give you a voice, a voice that you couldn't have had any other way. But I must admit that writing this book has actually left me with more questions than you gave me answers. I just wanted to get to know more about you, try to imagine things from your perspective. In reality it has blurred my mind and made me less certain about the few things I felt I really knew in the first place.

Would it have mattered if I hadn't had a go at doing this? Does anyone ever miss reading a book that hasn't been written? I doubt it, but I think the people out there should read something like this, something about someone like you. It would be good for them, and since you're not going to do it, I thought that I might.

So, were you happy with it? With the words and the style? I say style, as if I have consciously tried to concoct you in a deliberate way, to give you a clear and personalised voice that I think would suit you if you could actually speak. But to be honest the 'style', if that's the right word, seems to have just arrived really, it just seems to have come out of my knowing you and writing about you. So, the writing process itself kind of created you in book form, and your style seemed to be already there within the text as it appeared on the page. So, an utter fiction yes, but also a kind of representational truth. My truth about your truth, so perhaps somewhere in the middle, as best as we can really come to know it.

Perhaps we should all be a bit more relaxed about this first-hand reality thing anyway, and perhaps it helps when we realise that the words we use to describe what happens and the lived experiences we go through often don't really come that close to matching up, even when we are directly there to see it and describe it. But words are the only tools we have to do this kind of thing, actually writing a narrative account, and as you don't have any that you can give us, then the words used will just have to remain as mine.

Unfortunately, if I'm being honest, I don't think I have done too good a job with it all. There were times, many times really, when I was struck by the fact that the right words don't seem available to describe what I wanted to describe for you, as they were all mine, all coming from within me, formed in my type of personal reality, from my very individual experiences and understandings, not yours.

All that stuff about 'consciousness' and 'thoughts' and 'feelings' were way too general to convey what I wanted; the words I chose often either reductive or open to multiple misconception. I think that it is really unfortunate, but also probably inevitable, that you have been reduced by my description, with only a small part of you and your real experience being truly and fully represented and thus communicated to the reader. Yes, I'm so sorry about that.

I do realise that everything that I have written on your behalf is also very subjective and potentially, well actually, definitely open to contention. I do realise that, and although none of this is actually a lie, it is all partial and biased, and therefore basically untrue. But all I can say is that it is as true as I can make it, given all the limitations of all concerned; that's both me and you Harry, our limitations compounded - us bound together as equally unreliable witnesses.

But I do know one thing Harry, we certainly aren't just making this up, you and me, well certainly not you. We aren't trying to cheat anyone here. I really think that we are both doing our best to get this right, to show the world a bit of your kind of truth. Although perhaps we shouldn't be overly concerned about whether any of this is strictly true, or not. Instead, perhaps we should ask ourselves whether it is useful? Yeah, that will do, is it somehow useful? What do you think?

I sometimes wonder, admittedly not often, but I do sometimes wonder, when I am with you, about how much we really can share, even when we're doing the same thing together. It's just that, if you think about our own individual experiences, say me and you spending some time together, sitting looking back at each other doing your noises back to each other … well I sometimes wonder if that can ever be truly one shared experience or two individual ones, especially since we are so different. Are these moments actually shared? Are they one and the same for the both of us? Or are they two separate things entirely? And then I usually think (when I've looked up from my navel gazing) well does it really matter? Perhaps we should just do it, share it and enjoy it, whatever it is.

But you see I remember at your 40th birthday party. What a night that was. It was the full works: the balloons, the buffet supper, sausages on a stick, the lot, with banners, a disco, the flashing lights. All your staff team were there, and I shared a drink or two with them, and with you, to the sounds of the happy chatter and the disco music. And then there was the disco dancing. And actually, that's the bit that sticks in my mind the most, it was the bit that really made me think – not really at the time, it was just afterwards as I walked slowly and unsteadily home that I started to think of what a weird experience it must be to be taken for a dance, when you have such profound intellectual, perceptual and physical impairments.

You see, there you were having 'a dance' in your chair, facing forward, with your dancing partner pushing you from behind, all the sudden movements, you in your chair moving rapidly in one direction and then back again, twirling around, actually being twirled around, being jiggled from side to side, swerving around the other couples (the other couples all the same, one in a chair, one pushing from behind). From the outside it looked like a non-contact demolition derby for people in wheelchairs. All that, with the thumping full-volume disco sounds, and the flashing multi-coloured lights, all mixed together just because ABBA's 'Dancing Queen' came on the disco.

It all seemed perfectly fitting to watch at the time, it was only afterwards that I wondered how you had experienced it. I wondered if you had any feelings of losing control, of not being able to see who is pushing, and why they were pushing you, or ask them to stop. And the frantic twirling around; you certainly weren't doing the same thing, you weren't sharing the same experience they were, not by a long chalk. They were partying how they knew how to party. But you, you were being twirled and twisted and whatever. Goodness knows what you made of that involuntary 'shared' experience. Well maybe you really liked it, maybe it was just the right thing, maybe you actually like ABBA. I couldn't really tell, and of course you couldn't tell me either. But deep down I doubted it. Perhaps I should have said something. But sometimes it's really hard to do and say the right thing, especially if you don't know what the right thing to do and say actually is.

So perhaps I am trying to say something now, perhaps I am trying to find the right words and failing (not so different again, ehh) … a bit late I realise, but there it is. And here is your book.

So, bye for now Harry, see you around. Yes, definitely.

And sorry again about putting you to all this bother. You know, if you could actually read what I have written on your behalf, well, I wonder whether you would ever speak to me again, if you could actually speak that is.

Oh dear, is that a week and tasteless joke at your expense there Harry? Some people are very sensitive about that kind of thing. I don't mean anything by it, not really, but I bet if we could share such a joke, even a tasteless one, you Harry, you of all people would laugh, really laugh, right out loud. I bet you would, wouldn't you?

Harry?

Endnote:

Unfortunately, all the names (and sometimes even the gender) of all the fantastic people included in this book have had to be changed to protect their identity – it seems really mean, but apparently that's what we have to do.

So sorry H****y!

Cover Design by Oliver Firth

Printed in Great Britain
by Amazon

49844151R00109